TO ANCHOR A CLOUD
APPLY, APPLY, NO REPLY
A CLEAN BREAK

DILIP HIRO

TO ANCHOR A CLOUD
APPLY, APPLY, NO REPLY
A CLEAN BREAK

MADISON BOOKS

First Published in Great Britain in 1985 by
Madison Books, London.

Distributed by
Third World Publications,
151 Stratford Road, Birmingham B11 1RD. (021-773 6572)

Printed in Great Britain.

CONTENTS

PREFACE

To present history as drama is a formidable task. I discovered this the hard way: by actually trying to do it, without any previous experience in the art or craft of play-writing or theatre.

What got me going to write *To Anchor a Cloud* was the awareness that every school child in Britain and the Indian subcontinent is taught that the Taj Mahal is an outstandingly beautiful symbol of man's love for his woman, and that it was built by Shah Jahan, a Moghul emperor, for his wife, Mumtaz Mahal, after her death. Obviously Shah Jahan and Mumtaz Mahal were to be the leading characters of the work I proposed to write.

However, my research yielded very little about the personality of Mumtaz Mahal. So I had either to scrap the project or create the Mumtaz Mahal of my imagination. I chose the latter It proved to be a slow, frustrating process: it took the better part of three years to complete.

As a newcomer to imaginative writing I was much too cautious in using, what is commonly called, 'artistic licence'. This changed with time and practice — and the pressing need to produce a well formed, three act play, with each of the ten scene conveying a different mood. I realised that while existing within the bounds of historical events, my Mumtaz Mahal had to serve important dramatic functions.

If Mumtaz Mahal now emerges as a firm and logical person in comparison to her erratic and woolly-headed husband, this must be attributed as much to the demands of the dramatic form as to my own subversive tendencies. In retrospect, it seems, I sub-consciously wanted to subvert the prevelant (but erroneous) view of the Oriental woman, shrouded in veil, trailing behind her husband.

As it is, if properly produced and directred, *To Anchor a Cloud* should bring cheer to those who support the Women's Liberation Movement everywhere — be it the Western or Eastern bloc, or the Third World.

In the opinion of many familiar with India and Moghul history, my play has demythicized the great romantic couple of Moghul India. On the other hand, most of those unfamiliar with the country and its history may feel that I have presented the story romantically.

Anyway, there is nothing romantic about *Apply, Apply, No Reply*. It is a documentary work which tries to encapsulate the ambiance of a social order in a simple act: writing of an application for a job. Since the play is concerned with the very existence of the central character, Subodh Nayak, its resolution is bald. (Although written originally for television it transferred easily to the stage, without any alteration.)

On surface, *Apply, Apply, No Reply* — a threadbare play set in modern Calcutta — is totally different from the preceding episodic drama. But, underneath, the two works share a common trait: they challenge established views.

Just as I have tried to capture Subodh Nayak at a moment in his life when he is ripe for change, I have done so with Rachel Greene, an expatriate New Zealander settled in London, in *A Clean Break*. To quote a critic, it is a play about 'the politics of personal relationships'. It is a partly narrative work where the unfolding of the events of the earlier part of the day moves the play forward. By focussing on Rachel it tries to illustrate the dilemmas faced by Western women as they strive towards their social liberation.

To the extent that *A Clean Break* challenges the social status quo in Britain, and *Apply, Apply, No Reply*, does the political set-up in India, the two plays are subversive. One way to stress the common thread that unites them may lie in casting the same actor in the roles of Anil Roy and Anwar Hassan — with the latter literally leaving a cafe in Calcutta to appear in a London laundrette.

London, December 1984.   DILIP HIRO

TO ANCHOR A CLOUD
A Play in Three Acts

To
ROSHAN SETH

AUTHOR'S NOTE

As the play is set in the seventeenth century India a brief description of the Moghul dynasty, which then ruled the country, should help understand and appreciate it better. Jahangir was the Emperor of India from 1605 to 1627. He had four sons — Khusru, Parwez, Khurram and Shahriyar — in that order. Shah Jahan (literally, 'Ruler of the World') is the name that Prince Khurram acquired when he finally won the imperial throne. However, for the sake of simplicity, I have used the name Shah Jahan throughout the script. Since the Moghul dynasty lacked the tradition of the eldest son automatically succeeding the father, rivalry for the throne broke out during the ruling emperor's lifetime. This happened in the case of Jahangir and his sons. In 1618, when the play opens, the fight for the imperial throne was already on.

The main outline of the play is faithful to history. But to make drama out of history a playwright has to distort and recast some facts and events, and invent others, and I have done so.

Regarding the main characters, I have visualised them thus:

Jahangir: Forty-eight. Average height. A weak pale body with a handsome moustached face. A relaxed appearance. Moody with a quick changing mind; yet shrewdly aware of the interests of his Empire.

Nur Jahan: Favourite wife of Jahangir. Thirty-nine. Fair skinned, medium-sized, with an attractive face with prominent blue eyes. Energetic and ambitious. Domineering. Given to intrigue in her later days.

Shah Jahan: Twenty-seven. A good body; above average height. A darkish, bearded face with narrow, severe eyes. Sensitive, artistic, ambitious. His idealistic approach to life makes him prone to 'holier-than-thou' attitude. Devoted to Mumtaz Mahal. Fond of poetry, music and architecture; but also a valiant soldier.

Mumtaz Mahal: Favourite wife of Shah Jahan. Twentysix. An olive-coloured, well-proportioned figure with long black hair, a high brow, and large expressive eyes. Devoted to her husband without being servile or overbearing.

Asaf Khan: Father of Mumtaz Mahal, brother of Nur Jahan. Fortyeight. His slim, athletic body makes him look taller than he is. His grey bearded face is mellowed and serene. Flexible except in his unswerving loyalty to Mumtaz Mahal, and thus to Shah Jahan.

Parwez: Thirty-six. Stout with a bland , clean-shaven face. Slow in his movement and wits; but has zest for enjoyment.

Rodreguiz: A Jesuit priest. Forty-five. Large and florid; clean-shaven and bright eyed. Wily, with a special flair for striking bargains. Always dressed in black.

CHARACTERS
(In order of appearance)

JAHANGIR
EUNUCH
SHAH JAHAN
NUR JAHAN
PARWEZ
MUMTAZ MAHAL
MAIDSERVANT
ASAF KHAN
CHIEF NOBLE
FIRST NOBLE
SECOND NOBLE
EUNUCH
RODREGUIZ
PHYSICIAN
MESSENGER
STRANGER
FIRST EMISSARY
SECOND EMISSARY
FIRST MAID
SECOND MAID

TO ANCHOR A CLOUD

First presented at the Collegiate Theatre, London, on 25 September, 1970 by Ramesh Patel, with the following cast:

SHAH JAHAN	Saeed Jaffray
MUMTAZ MAHAL	Jamila Massey
JAHANGIR	Mohan Singh
NUR JAHAN	Pamela Salem
PARWEZ	Marc Zuber
ASAF KHAN	Dino Shafeek
RODREGUIZ	Marc Zuber
EUNUCH	Rafi Ameer
PHYSICIAN	Mohan Singh
CHIEF NOBLE	Mohan Parashar
FIRST NOBLE	Tariq Yunus
SECOND NOBLE	Ashwin Patel
MAIDSERVANT	Surinder Kochar
MESSENGER	Dino Shafeek
STRANGER	Mohan Parashar
FIRST EMISSARY	Ashwin Patel
SECOND EMISSARY	Avtar Chana
FIRST MAID	Surinder Kochar
SECOND MAID	Justine Elliot

NOBLEMEN, SOLDIERS, PRISONERS, SERVANTS

Directed by: Harbhajan Virdi

Designed by: Suresh Vedak

TO ANCHOR A CLOUD

ACT ONE

Scene 1 The Royal Tower in Agra; morning. 1618.
Scene 2 Shah Jahan's chamber; the same day.

ACT TWO

Scene 1 Open ground and a makeshift tent. 1624.
Scene 2 A tent; morning. A year later.
Scene 3 A tent; evening. Two years later.

ACT THREE

Scene 1 A courtyard in the Royal Fort, Agra. 1628.
Scene 2 The Royal Tower in Agra. Three years later.
Scene 3 The Royal Tower; several hours later.
Scene 4 Open space; a few hours later.

TO ANCHOR A CLOUD

ACT ONE

Scene I

Morning. The Royal Tower, Agra. It is richly decorated with paintings on the walls. Low platforms adjoining the walls are covered with mattresses and brightly coloured cushions. A large low table in the centre is laden with wine and fruits. JAHANGIR, dressed in bright silks and a bejewelled turban sits, sipping wine, while a palace EUNUCH, wearing a long shirt and tight pyjamas, attends.

JAHANGIR
(Holding up his goblet) How old did you say he is?
EUNUCH
Who, Your Majesty?
JAHANGIR
Shah Jahan. Who else? *(Gulps wine.)*
EUNUCH
(Nervous) I don't know, Your Majesty.
JAHANGIR
(Irritated) But you must have heard.
EUNUCH
(Nervous) Yes, yes...They say he is twenty-seven today.
JAHANGIR
More! *(Holds up his goblet)* Fill up the rest.
(Enter NUR JAHAN briskly.)
NUR JAHAN
(Thrusting out her hand) Look at the coins they're using! *(Throws the coins)* I thought they'd use the new coins — the ones embossed with my portrait.

JAHANGIR
(Blandly) Such were my orders. *(Examining the coins)* This is only silver.
NUR JAHAN
(Somewhat nervous) But it's the last weighing.

JAHANGIR

No. *(Quietly)* There's one more — in gold.

NUR JAHAN

Gold!

JAHANGIR

In gold coins with your portrait on them.

NUR JAHAN

(Pleased) Oh!

JAHANGIR

Yes. *(To the* Eunuch*)* Go, tell Prime Minister Asaf Khan to use only the new gold coins.

EUNUCH

Yes, Your Majesty.

JAHANGIR

And not to delay the prince once he's weighed.

EUNUCH

Yes...Your Majesty...
(Exits, muttering "Gold! Gold!".)

NUR JAHAN

But why are you weighing him in gold?

JAHANGIR

Well... the fact is *(undecided)*... well —

NUR JAHAN

(Impatient) Is that the excuse for putting my coins into circulation?

JAHANGIR

(After a moment of hesitation) Yes, yes. *(Enthusiastic)* The wider the circulation, the greater the fame.

NUR JAHAN

If only you'd tell me your plans in advance.
(Leaves briskly.)

JAHANGIR

(Aside) So that she could change them.
(Distant cries of 'Long live Royal Prince Shah Jahan!' – mixed with stray shouts of 'Gold' and noise of human stampede – grow near. JAHANGIR gets up and goes to the window.)
(Reflective) Put someone on top of a hill, and he's bound to

be shot down, with a hundred guns aimed at him. I love my Shah Jahan much too much. *(Pause)* I must keep them all guessing.

(Enter the EUNUCH.*)*

EUNUCH

His highness Royal Prince Shah Jahan!

(Enter SHAH JAHAN.*)*

JAHANGIR

Welcome and blessings, son.

SHAH JAHAN

(Bowing) This humble servant is most privileged to receive the royal blessing.

JAHANGIR

(Heartily) You deserve more than blessing. You're the worthiest of my sons.

SHAH JAHAN

A thousand thanks, father, for the compliment — and for having me weighed in gold. *(Pause)* I remain ever ready to serve the interest of the empire and of my lord-father.

JAHANGIR

Don't I know it? And haven't I given you the highest rank, the best chamber in the Royal Fort, married you to the most beautiful noble woman?

SHAH JAHAN

I'm forever obliged to you for your generosity, father — though *(hesitant)* – though I'd have gladly stopped at my very first marriage to Mumtaz Mahal.

JAHANGIR

Ah, my son, you love her dearly, I know. You always have. But the interest of the empire *(coughs)* come first. Every time a royal prince marries a princess or noble woman he strengthens the empire. So?

SHAH JAHAN

(Somewhat embarrassed) I didn't mean to question the wisdom of your action, father. Far from it. I was thinking of my weighing in gold this morning. Does that signify —

JAHANGIR

(Interrupting) Sit down.

SHAH JAHAN

Thank you, father.

JAHANGIR

(Offering him wine) Have some.

SHAH JAHAN

I'd rather not, father... I've never tasted wine before.

JAHANGIR

That's why you're so tense. Look at your brother Parwez, he drinks, he's relaxed.

SHAH JAHAN

But the edict of the Holy Quran forbid it.

JAHANGIR

They're flexible, *(chuckling)* as in my case. I've been exempted by the religious leaders of the Royal Court. *(Mimicking)* The burdens of the empire entitle the Emperor to relax in anyway he sees fit — so they've decreed.

SHAH JAHAN

(Stiffly) But Parwez —

JAHANGIR

Was exempted — by me. And I'm exempting you — now, for special occasions like today.

SHAH JAHAN

Does that mean —

JAHANGIR

(Firmly) Yes, now you can drink without any qualms.

SHAH JAHAN

(Still hesitant) Then... if that be the royal wish. Let me —

JAHANGIR

(Indicating a goblet) Take that.

(SHAH JAHAN *picks a goblet, then hands over another to* JAHANGIR. *Raising his goblet.)*

To your brilliant future! *(Sips.)*

SHAH JAHAN

(Staring at his drink) Yes... brilliant. *(After a moment of hesitancy, impetuously gulps the goblet down, grimaces, and breaks into a cough.)*

JAHANGIR

(Smiling) The first sip is never too pleasant — like the first

day on the imperial throne: very exciting yet very
uncomfortable.

SHAH JAHAN

Father!

JAHANGIR

(Quietly) Yes?

SHAH JAHAN

I feel something very special about today. *(Sips.)*

JAHANGIR

Of course, so you should.

SHAH JAHAN

(Emboldened, partly by drink) I mean, you too... how else?
...These references to the throne, my brilliant future,
weighing me in gold. *(Sips nervously)* I feel hopeful; I'm
ready.

JAHANGIR

(Mischievously) For another drink? *(Coughs.)*

SHAH JAHAN

(Tensed up) No, no. I mean Parwez was never weighed in
gold, not even on his thirtieth birthday. My tutor, Hakim
Jilani, is a very old man. *(Sips to avoid Jahangir's puzzled
look)* Very knowledgeable. He once told me about
weighings... no, not exactly... *(sips)* more about the
traditional significance of them than... I mean he said that
in our dynasty the fact of being weighed in gold has always
been inter... inter-preted as — *(Sips.)*

JAHANGIR

(Very quietly) Drink slowly.

SHAH JAHAN

(After a long draught) Yes, father.

JAHANGIR

When you drink slowly wine goes to the stomach and
soothes the body, but when you drink fast it goes to the
head: it arouses the imagination and fires ambition.
(Grimly) And ambition in a royal prince can be menacing.

SHAH JAHAN

(Sobered) I know.

JAHANGIR

Oh?

SHAH JAHAN

Yes, the fate of brother Khusru: blinded for life.

JAHANGIR

Blinded but alive. *(Coughs, then sips)* I wish he had known what lay under the glitter of the imperial throne: a bed of thorns. *(Coughs)* One problem is barely over when another arises: one rebellion is scarcely subdued when another erupts; then the famines, the rent-collections, the charities, the plots, the counter-plots, the intrigues; where does a man find his solace?

SHAH JAHAN

(Seriously) In the arms of his favourite wife.

JAHANGIR

Only if she is like Mumtaz Mahal, not like — *(Coughs.)*
(Enter NUR JAHAN briskly.)

NUR JAHAN

I heard coughing. *(Snatching the goblet from Jahangir's hand)* Enough. Remember the physician's warning : six more months of uncontrolled drinking — and coughing — and your condition will be beyond hope.

SHAH JAHAN

May Allah have mercy!

NUR JAHAN

Allah will have no mercy on those who have strayed from their faith. Who'd think this was the chamber of a Muslim, with all these infidel pictures?

JAHANGIR

(Protesting) This is art, not religion. *(Indicating Crucifixion)* Here's a man in pain, suffering. *(Indicating Mary and Jesus)* A mother with a child. *(To Nur Jahan)* A son. A pheasant more colourful than peacock. *(Pointing to Shah Jahan)* He'd appreciate that, being an artist at heart, and an architect, not you.

NUR JAHAN

Of course, I wouldn't. No true Muslim would. Representing life in pictures. This is idol worship.

SHAH JAHAN

(Holding a coin in his hand; meekly) And this?

NUR JAHAN

(Angered) You have no right to be disrespectful to the Empress. Or to take up valuable time of the Emperor while an urgent report awaits submission.

JAHANGIR

What is it now? Can't I have some rest on my son's birthday?

NUR JAHAN

(Taunting) I thought you wanted to be fully informed.

JAHANGIR

All right, say it.

NUR JAHAN

It's not for me to do so. Let Parwez himself do it.

JAHANGIR

Let him then.

NUR JAHAN

Shouldn't you receive him alone?

JAHANGIR

No. *(Mischievously)* He has nothing to hide from his younger brother, does he?

NUR JAHAN

How would I know? *(Claps her hands)* All I know is that the matter of his report is a delicate one.

(Enter PARWEZ dressed royally, though not as glamorously as Shah Jahan.)

PARWEZ

(Bowing before Jahangir) Lord-father, allow me the privilege to report that through my most secret investigations I have discovered that grave frauds are being committed by most of the Royal Court nobles. I possess unimpeachable evidence that though Sardar Ismat Khan, for example, receives the salaries every month of five thousand foot soldiers, and two thousand horsemen, he is in fact maintaining no more than 1,823 foot soldiers and 1,069 horses, 253 of which are, in fact large donkeys with clipped ears and coats painted with

henna. The latter fact was established by a thorough study of the excrement of the animals which my agents, dressed as grooms, collected in the royal stables. Furthermore, a detailed study of the manure itself revealed that the fodder administered to the royal horses falls well below the standards —

JAHANGIR

(Disgusted) Enough. To be discussing the state of manure just when I'm about to leave for a feast.

PARWEZ

A thousand pardons, lord-father.

JAHANGIR

(Hotly) Granting pardons won't help my appetite. *(Coughs.)*

SHAH JAHAN

(Truimphant) Father, could we continue our dialogue after the feast?

(While JAHANGIR continues to cough –)

NUR JAHAN

No! He has the Royal Council meeting to attend.

PARWEZ

(To Jahangir) I beg to submit furthermore on a matter more pleasant than —

JAHANGIR

(Exasperated) Please! Ah —

(Takes out a whistle from his pocket and blows. Enter the EUNUCH, running.)

(To the Eunuch, hotly) Who called for you?

EUNUCH

(Bowing) Your Majesty's orders: whenever the whistle blows I must present myself.

JAHANGIR

I cancel the order here and now. *(Brief pause)* Ask me tomorrow if the order remains cancelled. And close the window: the sun is much too bright *(Coughs.)*

EUNUCH

Yes, Your Majesty.

(Walks towards the window.)

JAHANGIR

(Rising to his feet) I blew the whistle to gain silence so that I could remember what I had forgotten. *(Shakes his head)* It's no use, I forget what it was I wanted to have announced after the feast. *(To* Shah Jahan*)* You look glum. Take this. It's a —

(Breaks into a cough. Resting his arm on the shoulders of SHAH JAHAN *and the* EUNUCH, *he exits.* NUR JAHAN *follows reluctantly.)*

PARWEZ

(Gulping wine) What exactly did he forget?

(He sees NUR JAHAN *re-enter; puts his goblet down.)*

NUR JAHAN

(Hotly) Why did you mention horse manure when I had told you not to? Every time I set up the situation for you, you spoil it with your crudeness.

PARWEZ

I'm sorry, mother. Very sorry. *(Pause)* His forgetting something, does that mean it didn't happen?

NUR JAHAN

No. I made sure those two didn't have much time together. But don't be misled by the Emperor's behaviour. His body may be failing but not his brain. He is far too clever for any one of us.

PARWEZ

But not clever enough to hide his partiality to Shah Jahan. *(Vehemently)* It's a scandal the way that dreamer of a prince squanders money on model buildings, hundreds of them, some in gold and silver, I've heard. Please, mother, tell the Emperor and the Royal Council of all his misdeeds, the ruin he'll bring if given a higher rank in the court.

NUR JAHAN

Of course, I will. But not crudely.

PARWEZ

(Gulping down a goblet of wine) I wish I could talk as glibly as Shah Jahan does. How he beguiles the Emperor with his discourses on art and architecture. But that won't get

him the throne, for it belongs to me. Me, the bravest of the princes.

NUR JAHAN

And the eldest, not counting the blinded Khusru.

Scene 2

The same day, afternoon. The chamber of Shah Jahan *in the Royal Fort, Agra. It is decorated in the style of the Royal Tower, except the walls, which are bare. On a low table, in the corner, lie models of various buildings.* MUMTAZ MAHAL, *wearing a long silken skirt and tight pyjamas, sits, eating grapes from a bowl, and humming. A whistle blows off-stage.* MUMTAZ MAHAL *stops eating momentarily, then continues.* SHAH JAHAN *enters with a whistle in his mouth. He blows it;* MUMTAZ MAHAL *covers her ears.*

MUMTAZ MAHAL

What is it?

SHAH JAHAN

(Contemptuous) A whistle: a European novelty. I was hoping to be named the Crown Prince. And what did I get? *(Blows the whistle out of frustration, then laughs bitterly)* A shiny little novelty. *(Drops it on a mattress.)*

MUMTAZ MAHAL

So it didn't happen.

SHAH JAHAN

How could it? He just sat there, guzzling wine as usual and talking.

MUMTAZ MAHAL

What about?

SHAH JAHAN

Oh, about the thousand and one problems facing the Emperor at all times. *(With sudden vehemence)* And he kept mentioning the number of wives he's got me. You know how much I hate talking about my other wives. *(Sadly)* It makes me feel as if I were a mere pawn.

(A MAIDSERVANT *enters, unnoticed, and slips behind a screen.)*

MUMTAZ MAHAL

(Sincerely) But the game is imperial, of the highest order.

SHAH JAHAN

(Bitterly) Only I'm not a player, just a pawn.

MUMTAZ MAHAL

You're a knight, my lord.

SHAH JAHAN

What good is a knight riding his charger, marching past the Emperor? No more than a grotesque puppet. The drums beat and cannons boom, but for whom? For the Emperor, who sits on his throne, in the balcony, far above his soldiers and subjects. No, what good is a knight? — or even a prince astride a horse?

MUMTAZ MAHAL

There were times when you rode an elephant.

SHAH JAHAN

Ah, those elephant fights! They were exhilarating *(Effusive)* You sit on top of an elephant, and look down: all men seem small, insignificant. You feel your chest swelling with power. Then the music begins, exciting music. Before you know it, your elephant is flailing his trunk and charging his rival — their trunks locked, they start pushing and pulling — and you, on top of your elephant, feel as if the very earth were quaking, the sun and the sky going round and round, and you feel afraid — yet, curiously enough, you're too excited to be afraid.

MUMTAZ MAHAL

I felt excited and afraid, as I sat at my window, watching every fight you fought. Every time you won, the harem hummed with praise for you.

SHAH JAHAN

But what use was that praise? Ephemeral. A fight is fought, won or lost, and is soon forgotten. No, I look for things that last — poetry, for example — or monuments.

(He goes to the models of the buildings.)

I like buildings, well-made buildings. So did Hakim Jilani. We'd spend hours talking about domes and minarets, panels and parapets, arches and beams. He thought of a monument as the solid form of a man's mood. He'd say a mosque should be built to awe the worshipper as if he were face to face with Allah; and a royal fort should have walls of rock with gardens and fountains inside — like two turtles held together belly-to-belly. He knew about buildings. And I'll build them all — the mosques, forts, palaces, whole cities. *(Pause. Softly)* But when?

MUMTAZ MAHAL
It'll be soon, my lord, very soon.

SHAH JAHAN
It better be soon, for time is running out. It takes years to build a palace or fort: it takes patience and planning. But magnify patience, and it becomes inaction. And inaction I hate. I see so much of it around me: the way the Emperor postpones succession.

MUMTAZ MAHAL
(Gingerly) He does face a delicate problem.He's probably finding it difficult to choose.

SHAH JAHAN
(Puzzled and hurt) But who's there to choose from? Shahriyar, the youngest, is just a boy. There is of course Parwez, who is older than me. But has he won as many battles as I have? Has he saved the Emperor's life? I did, on that hunting expedition by striking that ferocious tiger dead. And who informed the Emperor of the plot Khusru was hatching against him? There is no one else to beat my claims to the throne. *(Pause)* When is your father expected?

MUMTAZ MAHAL
After the Royal Council Meeting.

SHAH JAHAN
Oh, I wish the meeting were over soon. *(Anxiously)* He'll support my case, won't he?

MUMTAZ MAHAL
Certainly he will. Though, nowadays, he's not as influential as Nur Jahan. The Empress has your father

completely in her palm. But the Emperor won't live long, not with those asthmatic lungs. His eyes are failing too. He'll soon have to have leeches to suck the blood from the veins of his face.

SHAH JAHAN

Of all things, leeches? *(Vehement)* Leeches sucking blood. I've seen vultures pecking guts, jackals burrowing into corpses, their snouts red with blood; mad dogs tearing criminals apart and the elephants reducing men to pulp, without averting my eyes — but the one sight which makes me shiver is leeches sucking blood, until they're too bloated to suck any more and fall. Ahhh! *(Grimaces noisily.)*

MUMTAZ MAHAL

(Appealing) Please — let's not talk about something you hate so much. Please come, sit down. *(Caressing him)* Let me make a *paan* for you.

SHAH JAHAN

What do I need a *paan* for?

MUMTAZ MAHAL

It'll soothe your nerves.

SHAH JAHAN

My nerves are fine. *(Pause)* I think I'll, if you'll have one too.

MUMTAZ MAHAL

Yes, I will. *(Goes to the* paan *box)* Want a clove in yours?

SHAH JAHAN

No. *(*MUMTAZ MAHAL *brings him* paans *in a gold plate)* Which one?

MUMTAZ MAHAL

Whichever.

SHAH JAHAN

(Picking up his paan*)* I smell roses.

MUMTAZ MAHAL

(Chewing her paan*)* Because I used essence of roses.

SHAH JAHAN

(Chewing) There's no such thing.

MUMTAZ MAHAL

There is: so Nur Jahan claims. Her mother brought it for her on her return from Mecca. Nur Jahan sent me a whole bottle.

SHAH JAHAN

She does like you.

MUMTAZ MAHAL

Not as much as she used to.

SHAH JAHAN

Is that why she is sending you presents and giving you her best maidservant?

MUMTAZ MAHAL

I'm beginning to wonder. *(After some hesitation, intimately)* Lately, she has been rather overgenerous and that disconcerts me. I feel — I feel as if she's making up to me for something.

SHAH JAHAN

Oh Mumtaz, you have no reason to be suspicious of her. She may be rude and demanding with my father, but she has always been good to you, and to all her family.

MUMTAZ MAHAL

To her family, more than good. They can't thank her enough for all the favours she has lavished on them.

SHAH JAHAN

Nor can I — for having brought you to the Royal Fort.

MUMTAZ MAHAL

(Begrudging) Yes, she did bring us together, indirectly. *(Brief pause)* I'm sorry for speaking ill of her. Would you like to see the bottle of essence of rose she sent me?

SHAH JAHAN

Yes.

(MUMTAZ MAHAL brings out the bottle from inside the paan *box, then lifts its stopper.)*
(Sniffing) Hm... Heaven sent!

MUMTAZ MAHAL

I love the smell of roses.

SHAH JAHAN

And I love the woman who loves the smell of roses.

(Both laugh, then hug each other. Brief silence.)
Do you remember the rose bush near the fountain where we first met on that moonless night?

MUMTAZ MAHAL

Yes, you plucked a rose for me.

SHAH JAHAN

And I pricked my finger plucking it. But I didn't mind. It broke the trance I had been in since the moment I had caught sight of you crossing the threshold of your room, with your face bare. I thought I had seen an angel on earth — until — my glances crossed yours and you blushed, drawing the veil over your face.

MUMTAZ MAHAL

It was more than a blush on my face. The glance of those intense, brooding eyes had made my heart turbulent, my steps heavy: for a moment I was seized with an impulse to turn away from my palanquin, dash up to you and surrender, crying 'I'm yours, all yours'.

SHAH JAHAN

It sounds as if all that happened only a few days ago. *(Softly)* So much has happened since — my victories in the south, the birth of our children, my governorship of Gujarat. So much, yet so little. *(Loudly)* For what really matters has not happened.

MUMTAZ MAHAL

(Sincerely) What's that, my lord?

SHAH JAHAN

Do you need telling? You've always known my mind.

MUMTAZ MAHAL

Ssssh... my lord, I heard something.

SHAH JAHAN

You heard nothing but the beat of a heart in love with you. *(He gets up, agitated; paces for a while, then sits down next to her.)*
Tell me, Mumtaz, what should I do?

MUMTAZ MAHAL

Just wait.

SHAH JAHAN

Haven't I waited enough? *(Afterthought)* For your father, you mean? *(MUMTAZ MAHAL nods)* I wish he'd hurry.

MUMTAZ MAHAL

Ssssh...there! *(Pointing towards a screen)* Feet shuffling.
(SHAH JAHAN, rushing to the screen, bares his sword.)

SHAH JAHAN

Out! *(He jabs the screen with his sword.)*
Quick! Out!
(A woman, with her face and head covered with a scarf, emerges trembling.)
Speak, you wretch, before I —
(He pulls off her scarf.)

MUMTAZ MAHAL

(Shocked) The new maidservant! The one that the Empress sent us.
(The MAIDSERVANT falls to her knees.)

MAIDSERVANT

(To Shah Jahan) Mercy! Oh gracious prince, mercy!

SHAH JAHAN

(Pressing the sword against her throat) Mercy? For a spy?
(Shouts) For whom do you spy?

MAIDSERVANT

No, nobody. I came to put the baby to sleep.

SHAH JAHAN

Behind the screen?

MAIDSERVANT

Please spare my life, oh gracious prince!

MUMTAZ MAHAL

He may — if you tell us the truth.

MAIDSERVANT

I don't know... I just obey... obey the Empress...

SHAH JAHAN

(Puzzled) The Empress?

MAIDSERVANT

Yes, Her Majesty's orders, to report everything I saw or heard.

SHAH JAHAN

(Furious) You liar! Accusing the Empress of spying?

MAIDSERVANT

That's the truth, by the name of Allah and Holy —

SHAH JAHAN

That's a lie!

MAIDSERVANT

It's the truth: I'll swear by the Holy Quran. *(Pleading)* I'll be your slave for life, oh gracious prince. I'll tell you everything.

MUMTAZ MAHAL

About what?

MAIDSERVANT

The Empress... her plans... to marry her daughter to prince Shahriyar... her daughter by the previous husband.

SHAH JAHN

(Furious) Shut up! I'll have you thrown in a cauldron of boiling oil.

MAIDSERVANT

(Hysterical) No! No!

MUMTAZ MAHAL

Quiet!

(Enter ASAF KHAN *carrying a hooka in hand.)*

ASAF KHAN

Such shouting at this time of the day.

SHAH JAHAN

(Hotly) I'll silence her for ever. The punishment for spying is death.

ASAF KHAN

Spy, is she? *(Quietly)* Why kill her? Take her away from the Royal Fort along with your entourage.

SHAH JAHAN

(Surprised) Where to?

ASAF KHAN

To the unconquered parts of the continent.

SHAH JAHAN

Damn the continent! What about the succession?

ASAF KHAN

(Looking away) Let the unconquered parts of the continent be subdued first: that was the decision of the Royal Council.

SHAH JAHAN

(Bitterly) The Royal Council. But was it truly a royal decision, the one made by the Emperor?

ASAF KHAN

(With quiet sarcasm) Well, he signed the decree.

MUMTAZ MAHAL

(Sharply) Written and instigated by Nur Jahan, I suppose.

ASAF KHAN

Does it matter who wrote it? — or that the Emperor slept through the meeting? No. What matters is the royal seal. *(Indicates a ring on his hand to* Shah Jahan*)* Better get ready to leave soon.

SHAH JAHAN

(Confused) How can I? I mean, should I?....I mean can I afford to leave the court while Nur Jahan spreads her tentacles? *(To* Asaf Khan*)* Do you know that she's planning to marry her daughter by the first husband to Shahriyar?

ASAF KHAN

(Quietly) Yes, I overheard. *(To* Mumtaz Mahal, *persuasively)* You'll make him see reason, won't you?

MUMTAZ MAHAL

I'm not so sure.

ASAF KHAN

I am. *(To* Shah Jahan*)* Whenever in doubt, obey your superiors.

SHAH JAHAN

(Still upset) Oh, all the glib talk. I've just discovered a fresh rival in Shahriyar, as if Parwez were not enough. *(Paces)* What about Parwez?

ASAF KHAN

(Aborting a smile) Him? He too will be sent away — at the next meeting. To the farthest corner of the empire, as the governor of Bengal. That's my bargain with my sister, Nur Jahan.

SHAH JAHAN

(Sulking) Damn your bargains!

ASAF KHAN

Don't you see that this is your chance to realise your plans: conquer lands, and build your buildings.

SHAH JAHAN

Whose side are you on?

ASAF KHAN

(Hurt) Yours.

SHAH JAHAN

I wonder. *(Preparing to leave)* I sometimes wonder. *(Exits.)*

ASAF KAHAN

(Sadly) He's very bitter.

MUMTAZ MAHAL

For a good reason. You know well his claims to the throne.

ASAF KHAN

But merit alone is not enough. No royal prince, however brave and loyal, has ever been named Crown Prince by a ruling emperor of this dynasty.

MUMTAZ MAHAL

All the more reason for his excitement: to be the first in the dynasty to be so honoured.

ASAF KHAN

There are no firsts or lasts in this: a game without rules.

MUMTAZ MAHAL

There must be some.

ASAF KHAN

Only the ones that help a player to win. And sometimes to win, one must stand still, or move aside or even step back.

MUMTAZ MAHAL

You've told me that often.

ASAF KHAN

But you haven't told your husband often enough.

MUMTAZ MAHAL

I have. I really have. But it doesn't seem to work.

ASAF KHAN

Make it work, this time, for his sake — and ours. Make him swallow his disappointment, and march southward.

MUMTAZ MAHAL

On one condition.

ASAF KHAN

Which is...

MUMTAZ MAHAL

That you inform us of Nur Jahan's every single move.

ASAF KAHN

That's the least I can do for my daughter. *(Hugging her)* My lovely daughter.

ACT TWO

Scene 1

Some years later; central India. Open ground. Martial music, off-stage. War cries rise, then subside. SHAH JAHAN *in armour – followed by nobles, bearing arms and shouting 'Long live Emperor Jahangir!' – walks acorss the stage. Lights dim. Then shouts of 'Long live Emperor Jahangir!' followed by 'Onward to Berar!' off-stage. Martial music. War cries. Brief silence.* SHAH JAHAN *enters, stage-right; nobles enter, stage-left, followed by prisoners with bound wrists.*

CHIEF NOBLE
(Stepping forward) The prisoners are here.
SHAH JAHAN
(Imperious) So I see.
CHIEF NOBLE
(Indicating) The Chief Minister of —
*(*FIRST NOBLE *pushes the prisoner.)*
SHAH JAHAN
Follow the protocol. First the King.
CHIEF NOBLE
(Bowing) He isn't here, Your Highness.
SHAH JAHAN
Why? Is he dead?
CHIEF NOBLE
No, he's hiding.
SHAH JAHAN
Then find him.
CHIEF NOBLE
(Awkwardly) He's hiding in a mosque, your —
SHAH JAHAN
Mosque? But he isn't a Muslim.
CHIEF NOBLE
But he became one: he circumcised himself.
SHAH JAHN
Oh, the cheat! The scoundrel. Surround all mosques!

CHIEF NOBLE

There's only one.

SHAH JAHAN

Only one? Only one mosque in such a large town. How many Muslims in this town?

CHIEF NOBLE

I ...I haven't asked.

SHAH JAHAN

(Louder) How many Muslims in this town?

SECOND NOBLE

(Stepping forward) Eleven thousand. Your Highness.

SHAH JAHAN

Eleven thousand — and only one mosque! This is outrageous. *(To the* Chief Noble*)* Build another mosque. *(The* CHIEF NOBLE *bows)* Large enough to take in all eleven thousand Muslims.

(Murmurs of awe – 'Eleven thousand!' 'Eleven thousand!' – arise.)

FIRST NOBLE

(Dissenting quietly) A mosque for eleven thousand? But the design —

SHAH JAHAN

I have the model.

FIRST NOBLE

The cost.

SHAH JAHAN

That doesn't matter. What matters is the glory of Islam, and building a place for the worship of Allah.

(Fresh murmurs of 'Glory!' 'Mosque for eleven thousand!'.)

Stop murmuring. *(Pause)* Haven't you seen a mosque for eleven thousand?

CHIEF NOBLE

No, Your Highness.

SECOND NOBLE

I've not even dreamt of one so vast.

SHAH JAHAN

That's the pettiness of your dreams, for dreams will go as far as you take them. Dreams come first, reality later. Try and imagine a mosque for eleven thousand: why eleven, why not twenty, or thirty or even a hundred thousand? *(All present turn to* Shah Jahan*, open mouthed.)*

CHIEF NOBLE

These are the vision of angels — and prophets.

SHAH JAHAN

No, the visions of mortals with enough courage to imagine them. Courage and imagination, my soldiers! Oceans can be crossed, mountains moved, and clouds brought down with courage and imagination. And faith — in Allah, in Prophet Mohammed, and the Moghul Empire!

SECOND NOBLE

(Raising his sword) Long live!

ALL

(Except FIRST NOBLE*)* Prince Shah Jahan!

SHAH JAHAN

No! I'm but a servant of the Emperor. Long live!

ALL

Emperor Jahangir!

SHAH JAHAN

To celebrate my victory I'll build an imperial palace on the highest hill in this kingdom.

FIRST NOBLE

On top of a hill?

SHAH JAHAN

(Poetic) Yes, on the very top, so that at night when it's lit with a thousand lamps it'll be seen for miles around — a beacon of the Moghul Empire!

(Lights fade quickly as SHAH JAHAN *and others exit. Darkness for a while. When lights reappear they reveal a makeshift tent with a window and a latticed screen on each side.* SHAH JAHAN *sits on a mattress, lost in his thoughts, while* MUMTAZ MAHAL, *a snuff-box in hand, stands by. Late afternoon.)*

MUMTAZ MAHAL

Would you like some, my lord?

SHAH JAHAN

(Absently) What?

MUMTAZ MAHAL

Snuff. *(Takes some.)*

SHAH JAHAN

Hmm...

MUMTAZ MAHAL

It does clear stuffed-up nostrils. *(No response)* What are you thinking, my lord?

SHAH JAHAN

I'm thinking of the chaos in Parwez's province. It pleases me no end. What better proof does the Emperor need of Parwez's incapacity to rule?

MUMTAZ MAHAL

Yes — that's if the situation there is as bad as you've been told.

SHAH JAHAN

Isn't it?

MUMTAZ MAHAL

I don't know. What I know is that these oral messengers have-a-certain-tendency-to-twist — *(Sneezes)* —

SHAH JAHAN

(Irritated) Have what?

MUMTAZ MAHAL

(Slowly) A certain tendency to twist the news so as to please the prospective hearer, you see.

SHAH JAHAN

No, I don't. There never has been any doubt about Parwez being worthless. Did the messenger twist the news about my soldiers and nobles too?

MUMTAZ MAHAL

They couldn't, even if they tried. It seemed you were, in a way, expecting that news.

SHAH JAHAN

Was I? *(Sarcastic)* I was expecting my men to go looting and raping when every day I exhort them to obey the rules of proper conduct.

MUMTAZ MAHAL

It's the first time some of them let their jubilant mood get the better of them. They've fought two major battles with you, and won. I often wonder how soldiers manage without women. It must be hard on them.

SHAH JAHAN

It isn't easy fighting for the glory of my dynasty and my future. They ought never to forget that. If they do, they must pay for it. Heavily.

MUMTAZ MAHAL

You are not going to hang them?

SHAH JAHAN

Yes, I am.

MUMTAZ MAHAL

You'll only be weakening your forces, my lord.

SHAH JAHAN

But enhancing my standing , in the eyes of justice.

MUMTAZ MAHAL

Please think of the desertions that might follow these executions.

SHAH JAHAN

Better a few moral men than a horde of immoral ones.

MUMTAZ MAHAL

Not when we're moving further and further from the capital. *(Pause. Appealing)* Let's stop here for a while — please.

SHAH JAHAN

No, we can't; we must go on. *(Goes to the window)* I must keep on conquering territories until there's no land left, and I stand by the sea *(Brooding)* I like the sea; I like its enormity.

MUMTAZ MAHAL

It terrifies me.

SHAH JAHAN

It fascinates me, excites me. *(Suddenly firm)* But that's not the point. Each victory to my credit is a step nearer to the throne.

MUMTAZ MAHAL
(Pulling out a cartridge from her side pocket) One trick like this cancels out a dozen victories.

SHAH JAHAN
What's that? An amulet?

MUMTAZ MAHAL
No, a report from my father: Nur Jahan married her daughter to Shahriyar — secretly.

SHAH JAHAN
(Upset) Did she? *(He grabs the cartridge, reads the note)* What's to be done then? Your father says nothing.

MUMTAZ MAHAL
(Quietly) That would have been unwise of him — in his own handwriting. Even carrier-pigeons get intercepted sometimes. But you know what I suggested. Let's drag our feet a bit.

SHAH JAHAN
It might be better to ignore the news altogether and keep on as before, hoping that something would turn up in my favour, sooner or later. It might. *(Brief pause)* It's quite likely, after that sign I had.

MUMTAZ MAHAL
What sign? When?

SHAH JAHAN
Last night, I was too excited to sleep after that news about Parwez. I got out of bed. As I was leaving the tent, I looked up: I saw a star falling. It was sudden, very sudden, but I managed to tie a knot in my shirt string. I did it before the star vanished. That's an omen which never proves wrong.

MUMTAZ MAHAL
If our wishes were fulfilled through signs, we wouldn't have lost our baby. All the charms and amulets we bought for him.

SHAH JAHAN
(Vehemently) I did not buy anything. I saw a sign from the heavens above.

MUMTAZ MAHAL
(Lightly) That stubborn optimism —

SHAH JAHAN
Which will be borne out sooner than you think. We'll have good news before the Emperor moves to Kashmir for the summer.

MUMTAZ MAHAL
While we roast in the scorching south, travelling endlessly.

SHAH JAHAN
(Apologetic) I know, Mumtaz, and I sympathise. *(Hugging her)* You had better rest now. I have to inspect the camp.

MUMTAZ MAHAL
Sometimes I wish a disaster would strike us, and shake us out of our smugness.

SHAH JAHAN
If it be Allah's will.

MUMTAZ MAHAL
Will you be seeing the Chief Noble?

SHAH JAHAN
Yes. Why?

MUMTAZ MAHAL
Do please ask him to get some ice for me. There are mountains not too far from here.

SHAH JAHAN
They are not high enough for snow.
(Enter EUNUCH.)

EUNUCH
His Excellency the Chief Noble Jaffar Khan!

SHAH JAHAN
Let him come.
(As the CHIEF NOBLE enters, MUMTAZ MAHAL slips behind a latticed screen.)
You are early.

CHIEF NOBLE
(Bowing) Yes, Your Highness. There arrived a most urgent decree for the Royal Court.
(He delivers the decree. SHAH JAHAN unseals it and reads.)

SHAH JAHAN

Wait outside.

(As the CHIEF NOBLE *exits,* SHAH JAHAN *goes to the latticed screen.)*

Mumtaz!

*(*MUMTAZ MAHAL *emerges from behind the screen.)*

What did I tell you? Here's the proof — a royal decree signed and sealed, not a cryptic note carried by pigeons or oral messages twisted... Read it!

MUMTAZ MAHAL

(Fidgeting with the decree, reading) 'The Emperor is pleased to...'

SHAH JAHAN

Not that, the next paragraph.

MUMTAZ MAHAL

(Reading) 'And so your are hereby ordered to attack the land and forces of Parwez who through his persistent refusal to obey the royal decrees has earned himself the odious title of "Rebellious Prince", and stands charged with treason against the Emperor...'

SHAH JAHAN

Parwez charged with treason and a royal order for me to destroy my one and only serious rival. My sign, my star!

MUMTAZ MAHAL

(Wondering aloud) How did this happen?

SHAH JAHAN

How are the just and conscientious rewarded by Allah? How? He has His ways, mysterious ways.

(He blows the whistle. The EUNUCH *enters.)*

Call the Chief Noble. We're marching northeast to squash Parwez. *(Baring his sword)* Squash!

EUNUCH

Yes, Your Highness. *(Exits.)*

MUMTAZ MAHAL

Now at last you have a convincing reason to free your offending nobles and soldiers: to fight Parwez for you.

SHAH JAHAN

(Haughtily) On the contrary. With more troops coming from the capital, I can do without them.

Scene 2

A year later; eastern India. Early dawn. A makeshift tent. SHAH JAHAN, restless, goes to the window. In the distance a muezzin calls. MUMTAZ MAHAL emerges from behind a screen.

SHAH JAHAN

The muezzin does have a powerful voice.

MUMTAZ MAHAL

(Yawning) Loud enough to wake up the indolent.

SHAH JAHAN

I envy the Muslims living west of Mecca; they pray facing east. It must be wonderful to face east in the morning, to see the sun stretch its thousand arm slowly, luxuriantly, up above the horizon, gradually filling the sky with its orange radiance.

MUMTAZ MAHAL

(Standing behind him) The sky is like a vast curtain dyed with henna.

SHAH JAHAN

So peaceful, the lull before the battle. Two more sunsets before I meet Parwez.

MUMTAZ MAHAL

Not so soon.

SHAH JAHAN

Why not?

MUMTAZ MAHAL

The reinforcements, my lord. The reinforcements from the capital haven't arrived yet.

SHAH JAHAN

Ah, they'll come.

MUMTAZ MAHAL

They should have been here a fortnight ago.

SHAH JAHAN

Surely, one can't expect a cavalry of twentyfive thousand to march two thousand miles without losing a few days. They'll soon be here.

MUMTAZ MAHAL

Supposing they are not?

SHAH JAHAN

They've *got* to be here: the prestige of the Royal Court is involved.

MUMTAZ MAHAL

But even royal forces can get bogged down by a swollen river, or torrential rain...or get intercepted...or —

SHAH JAHAN

In that case we do nothing: just stay where we are. *(Brief pause)* There is, in fact, very little else I can do: to the northeast are the forces of Parwez; to the west the only road to capital; and to the east, facing the sea, the Christian colony.

MUMTAZ MAHAL

(Reflecting) The Christians?

SHAH JAHAN

Yes, the plunderers, the ones who abducted your maids. I wish you hadn't advised me against punishing them.

MUMTAZ MAHAL

Why waste energy beating the cat for drinking your milk when a wolf is snarling at you? No, I don't regret my advice. In a way, I'm glad we haven't alienated them: they could be useful.

SHAH JAHAN

How?

MUMTAZ MAHAL

They have skilled gunners in their colony.

SHAH JAHAN

You are not suggesting that I employ them?

MUMTAZ MAHAL

I think I am.

SHAH JAHAN

You surprise me. To invite Christians to meddle in the affairs of a Muslim empire?

MUMTAZ MAHAL

Don't let them meddle. Buy them for money, use them and throw them away like the kernels of dates.

SHAH JAHAN

Who's got the money to buy them? After all the battles I've fought, and the mosques and palaces I've built. And not a silver coin from the imperial treasury since we left the capital.

MUMTAZ MAHAL

Promising money is not the same as paying it.

SHAH JAHAN

Now you're proposing a breach of promise by me.

MUMTAZ MAHAL

But only with those notorious for plundering.

SHAH JAHAN

Must we, Muslims, too lower ourselves?

MUMTAZ MAHAL

(Exasperated) Oh, my lord, if only you'd — *(Tails off.)*

SHAH JAHAN

Mumtaz...

MUMTAZ MAHAL

I'm only thinking of your interests, how best to serve you.

SHAH JAHAN

All right. I'll do something, if that'll please you. I'll consult my astrologer.

MUMTAZ MAHAL

(Testily) Astrologers, astrologers, while there's a major crisis brewing. *(Examining her tongue in a mirror)* My mouth... feels slimy. *(Sits down)* I don't feel well.

SHAH JAHAN

Let me call the physician.

MUMTAZ MAHAL

No, no, please. Just a spittoon. *(Spits in the spittoon)* Don't worry, please. I'll be all right. This is quite normal — really.

SHAH JAHAN

Normal? Sickness in the morning normal? *(Suddenly realizing)* Oh, my Mumtaz! *(Hugs her)* Is it true? *(MUMTAZ MAHAL nods)* Another baby. *(Hugs her)* Oh, the grace of Allah! It'll be a son this time.

MUMTAZ MAHAL

(Bitterly) If he lives.

SHAH JAHAN

I'm certain he will. You better lie down — or... gargle with lime-water.

(He helps MUMTAZ MAHAL to get up and walk towards the screen, then returns to the window. Facing west, raising his hands in prayer.)

Oh Allah, forgive her for losing faith: I seek forgiveness for her. And for myself too: as I, too, am beginning to doubt. The royal reinforcements haven't arrived, and the time for battle is drawing near. I need courage and faith more than ever, and above all, I need men and materials. *(Looking out)* Not a cloud of dust, not a horse in sight.

(Enter the EUNUCH running.)

EUNUCH

(Breathless) The scouts... the scouts have brought news: the forces of Parwez are on the march.

SHAH JAHAN

(Surprised) Already? How many?

EUNUCH

Fifty thousand foot soldiers, thirtyfive thousand cavalry, Your —

SHAH JAHAN

Thirtyfive thousand cavalry! Beat the drum of alarm. Rush!

EUNUCH

Yes, Your Highness. *(Prepares to leave.)*

SHAH JAHAN

Get the Christian leader. Quick!

EUNUCH

Which first, Your —

SHAH JAHAN

(Frantic) Both at once.

EUNUCH

(Confused) Both? *(Brief pause)* Yes, this moment.
(He leaves.)

MUMTAZ MAHAL

(Muttering from behind the screen) At last he's beginning
to learn.

*(SHAH JAHAN paces nervously. MUMTAZ MAHAL
emerges, unnoticed, from behind the screen.)*

SHAH JAHAN

(Muttering) How did Parwez know? He was not supposed
to... he was not supposed to know our plans, our
movements.

MUMTAZ MAHAL

The rumours, the spies.

SHAH JAHAN

(Excited) But he's marching. He's marching against the
Imperial Crown: the fool! *(Puzzled)* How did he get thirtyfive
thousand horsemen? I have no more than ten thousand,
and battle weary at that.

MUMTAZ MAHAL

If only you hadn't executed your own soldiers.

SHAH JAHAN

Only a few immoral men.

MUMTAZ MAHAL

But the hundreds of desertions that followed.

SHAH JAHAN

It's too late now.

MUMTAZ MAHAL

It's never too late to learn from past mistakes.

SHAH JAHAN

(Snapping) This is hardly the time...

MUMTAZ MAHAL

Any time!

*(Angered, SHAH JAHAN first looks away, then drifts
down-stage.)*

(Getting closer to Shah Jahan) I'm sorry, my lord; I didn't
mean to be curt.

SHAH JAHAN
(Quietly) Neither did I. *(Brief pause)* My temper is short today.

MUMTAZ MAHAL
I understand. The situation is grave.

SHAH JAHAN
That's no reason for me to lose my temper. Not with you, anyway. *(Caressing her)* I want you to stand by me.

MUMTAZ MAHAL
(Hugging him) I always have, and always will.

SHAH JAHAN
Sometimes I wonder if I'm not being too presumptious about you, taking you for granted; but I don't mean to. I thank Allah daily for having given me you, the gem of the Empire, a pearl of beauty, a faithful wife and an ideal mother for my children.

MUMTAZ MAHAL
You'll spoil me with your flattery.

SHAH JAHAN
You're beyond spoiling.

MUMTAZ MAHAL
No one is. *(She disengages herself.)*

SHAH JAHAN
You are, I am sure of that. *(Pause)* I wish I could be half as sure of myself, about my loyalty to my principles. I'm beginning to doubt. I prayed for strength and fortitude earlier.

MUMTAZ MAHAL
There's more strength in one cannon than in a hundred prayers.
(Enter the EUNUCH.)

EUNUCH
Padre Roza Raik is here, Your Highness. The Christian leader.

SHAH JAHAN

Let him come.

(The EUNUCH *leaves.* MUMTAZ MAHAL *withdraws behind the screen.* SHAH JAHAN *steps on to a dais. Enter* RODREGUIZ.*)*

RODREGUIZ

(Raising his hand) Greetings!

SHAH JAHAN

(Annoyed) Just greetings? No bowing, not even a nod. *(Loudly)* I want the two slave girls back by sunset.

RODREGUIZ

(With feigned surprise) Slave girls? What slave girls?

SHAH JAHAN

You're a poor liar, padre. *(Loudly)* The ones your followers abducted from our camp three days ago.

RODREGUIZ

(Hurt) That's a grave accusation. We, Christians, stealing? *(Firmly)* There are no slave girls in our colony.

MUMTAZ MAHAL

(From behind the screen) We'll let you keep them.

RODREGUIZ

(After the initial shock) I don't understand. Will you?

SHAH JAHAN

(Harshly) Only if you help us.

RODREGUIZ

In what way?

SHAH JAHAN

By supplying us with artillery.

RODREGUIZ

To fight whom?

SHAH JAHAN

(Solemnly) To fight the evil designs of Parwez: such are the orders of the Emperor.

RODREGUIZ

(Doubtful) Oh?

SHAH JAHAN

Yes, they are. Do you doubt it?

RODREGUIZ

Well —

SHAH JAHAN

Look! *(Pulls the royal decree out of his pocket.)*
Read this.
(RODREGUIZ moves forward, and looks at the decree.)

RODREGUIZ

I know nothing of decrees: this could be forged.

SHAH JAHAN

(Furious) Are you accusing the Crown Prince of forgery?

RODREGUIZ

(Definat) Nothing of the sort. It's all very confusing. Only
this morning I heard a company of soldiers with the royal
colours shouting 'Long live Royal Prince Parwez!'. They
had cannons.

SHAH JAHAN

(Tensing to cover his alarm) Those are meant for me, sent
by the Emperor.

RODREGUIZ

(With a sardonic smile) But they were shouting 'Long live
Royal Prince Parwez!'

SHAH JAHAN

You heard wrong.
(RODREGUIZ shrugs his shoulders.)
Don't go by rumours. Listen, padre, I'll pay you well.

RODREGUIZ

(Suddenly interested) Yes?

SHAH JAHAN

Very well. All gold and silver... *(Throwing him a necklace)*
Take this... for now... rubies and diamonds later.
(RODREGUIZ catches the necklace.)

RODREGUIZ

(Using the necklace as a rosary) Oh Lord, thou art in
heaven... lead us not to temptation... deliver us... *(Loudly)*
We have to face cannons, you know.

SHAH JAHAN

(Throwing him a crown ruby) And this...
(RODREGUIZ examines the ruby greedily.)

SHAH JAHAN
It's the most valuable ruby in the whole empire.

RODREGUIZ
It seems —

SHAH JAHAN
(Anxious) How soon will you have the gunners ready?

RODREGUIZ
(Tepidly) It will take time. They have to clean the cannons, oil them, practise target-shooting, and then —

SHAH JAHAN
(Impatient) All right, all right, hurry back. My eunuch will lead you out. *(About to blow the whistle.)*

RODREGUIZ
No need for that. I'll slip away through the back — but not as a Christian padre.
(He drops his Jesuit robe, revealing a Muslim alem's - religious leader's - dress. Rushes out.)

MUMTAZ MAHAL
(Emerging from behind the screen) Clever! Very clever! How are we to rely on a person like that?

SHAH JAHAN
(Without conviction) The lure of more money will draw him back.

MUMTAZ MAHAL
I hope it does. I'm no longer sure that he's a Christian, or that he came from the Christian colony.

SHAH JAHAN
(Fighting his own doubts) Please, Mumtaz, don't let fear cloud your judgement.

MUMTAZ MAHAL
I'm not afraid.

SHAH JAHAN
Nor am I.
(Stray shots are heard off-stage.)
What was that? *(Nervous)* The forces of Parwez? Oh Allah! My helmet. Let me have my helmet! And armour too.
(MUMTAZ MAHAL leaves.)

No no, don't leave. This is unheard of. I've been tricked, taken by surprise. Battles have to be arranged, grounds chosen, ceremonies performed... this is unheard of... in our dynasty.

(MUMTAZ MAHAL and a MAIDSERVANT enter, carrying armour. Panic, off-stage.)

Hurry!

(Enter the EUNUCH.)

EUNUCH

A messenger with a white flag, Your Highness.

(Enter the MESSENGER.)

MESSENGER

Such panic! To fire at me just because I wasn't riding a white horse as well. *(Bowing)* I bear a message from His Highness Prince Parwez.

SHAH JAHAN

Is it to fix the date and time for the battle?

MESSENGER

No. His Highness wishes to meet Your Highness — privately.

SHAH JAHAN

(Haughtily) What's there to meet for? To talk to a rebel of the empire?

MESSENGER

(Firmly) His Highness wishes to avoid bloodshed.

SHAH JAHAN

(Impetuously) Don't we all?

MUMTAZ MAHAL

Then let him come, with one bodyguard only.

(The MESSENGER looks from Mumtaz Mahal to Shah Jahan and back. SHAH JAHAN, after moments of hesitation, nods reluctantly. The MESSENGER bows and leaves.)

SHAH JAHAN

(To the Eunuch) Better have the white flag unfurled.

EUNUCH

Yes, Your Highness.

(The EUNUCH *exits.* SHAH JAHAN *steps on the dais.
Sounds of a mob gathering, off-stage. Enter* PARWEZ
followed by a bodyguard in armour.)

SHAH JAHAN

Why do you confuse the people by flaunting the royal
colours?

PARWEZ

Who's confusing who? I have royal orders to bring you to
the Court. Look! *(Flaunts a decree)* Only I wish to avoid
bloodshed.

SHAH JAHAN

(Flaunting his decree) I have royal orders to quell your
rebellion.

PARWEZ

(Amused and incensed) Me, rebelling? Me, Royal Prince
Parwez, awarded the highest rank in our dynasty: the rank
of forty thousand cavalry and fifty thousand foot soldiers.
Me, rebelling? Why, I never heard anything more
ridiculous. *(Solemnly)* Now, surrender yourself, Prince
Shah Jahan, and save me the odious task of reading out
the long list of your crimes against the Royal Court. *(Pause)*
No? *(Pause)* Very well, then. *(Looking at the decree)* The
charge-sheet against you is much too long, and my voice is
hoarse from singing and shouting. You're my brother, I
don't like doing this. But duty —

SHAH JAHAN

(Sarcastic) Duty?

PARWEZ

(Very solemnly) Yes, duty, that sense of proper conduct
which separates princes from people. Now listen. *(Reads)*
Since you left the capital four years ago, you've lavished
money on your friends and flatterers, built palaces that
were not needed, laid roads and dug wells that were not
authorised. And, *(loudly)* hear this; you slaughtered — yes
slaughtered — a posse of valiant nobles and soldiers of the
Empire under false accusations of rape and loot. That is not
all. You went about holding poets' conferences and doling
out money to whosoever called himself an artist or

architect. Killing warriors and rewarding architects: to
what depth have you dragged our glorious dynasty?

SHAH JAHAN

(Protesting) Not a word about the mosques I've built.

PARWEZ

Only one, for a hundred Muslims.

SHAH JAHAN

No, for eleven thousand.

PARWEZ

Exactly, extravagance! We had detailed reports — from
him.
*(Indicates his bodyguard, who removes his helmet,
revealing himself to be the former* FIRST NOBLE *of* Shah
Jahan.)

SHAH JAHAN

(Shocked) You? Of all people, you! How are you alive? I
ordered your execution for indulging in looting and raping.

FIRST NOBLE

By Allah's grace, I live. It was my mission to tell the truth
about your actions: they've upset the Royal Court. Empress
Nur Jahan is furious.

SHAH JAHAN

(Hotly) Nur Jahan? That old scheming...

PARWEZ

Careful, not a word against the Empress.

MUMTAZ MAHAL

(To Parwez*)* Can't you see through Nur Jahan's plans? Now
that she has married her daughter to Prince Shahriyar she
wants both of you out of the way. She's playing you two
against each other.

PARWEZ

Both of you smell of treason. Now, you're enticing me to
rebel against the Empire.

MUMTAZ MAHAL

(Vehemently) Don't identify the Empire with her. She's no
more than an ambitious noblewoman plotting for power.
Can't you see that?

PARWEZ

(Sarcastic) All I see is another woman meddling in the affairs of the Empire.

SHAH JAHAN

(Baring his sowrd) Careful, before you say another word against my wife.

(Flourish of trumpets. Drums sound. SHAH JAHAN *and* PARWEZ *cross swords. As the fight progresses, the stage is cleared. War cries, off-stage. Cannons boom.* SHAH JAHAN *runs off. War cries subside. Lights fade.* SHAH JAHAN *reenters, running and stops.* PARWEZ *enters, followed by his nobles. Brief skirmish between* SHAH JAHAN *and* PARWEZ. SHAH JAHAN *runs off.)*

PARWEZ

Once again he slipped away. The devious wretch. But *(swings his sword)* one day I'll get him. Get him, and run my sword through him.

Scene 3

Two years later; southern India. A makeshift tent. Evening. MUMTAZ MAHAL *helps* SHAH JAHAN *to sit up in bed. The low table by the side of the bed, is crowded with bottles and bowls.*

MUMTAZ MAHAL

Does that feel better, my lord?

SHAH JAHAN

(Listlessly) I think so. *(Moans)* Does it matter what I think?

MUMTAZ MAHAL

Of course it does — to me, to all your followers.

SHAH JAHAN

What followers? *(Grunts)* Even your father has forsaken me.

MUMTAZ MAHAL

He hasn't. It's simply the carrier pigeons can't fly over the mountains of Kashmir.

SHAH JAHAN

Why isn't the Emperor returning to the capital? Could it be — *(tails off.)*

MUMTAZ MAHAL

Yes, his condition must be serious.

SHAH JAHAN

What comfort does that bring to me? A fugitive in the south, harassed by Parwez. *(Moans)* And my illness —

MUMTAZ MAHAL

It's nothing serious, my lord.

SHAH JAHAN

That's precisely what I told my physician yesterday when he came with leeches to suck my blood. Leeches! *(Grimaces.)*
(The PHYSICIAN is poised to enter.)

MUMTAZ MAHAL

He's without choice, the poor man.
(She signals to the PHYSICIAN, who enters quietly with a bowl in hand.)

SHAH JAHAN

But mine is a special case.

PHYSICIAN

The treatment is still the same, Your Highness. Swollen veins of blood, and leeches to empty them.

SHAH JAHAN

(Exasperated) The same, the same, ever since I've been sick you've been wanting my blood. Why?

PHYSICIAN

(For the nth time) In this kind of sickness the patient —

SHAH JAHAN

I've heard all that. Lies! You sell royal blood, don't you? I know you do.

PHYSICIAN

(Nervous) Your Highness...

SHAH JAHAN

How much do you get for it? *(Shouting)* How much?

PHYSICIAN

Nothing; no, no. *(Improvising)* Royal blood is much too precious... no one'd dream... of asking. It can't be valued...

MUMTAZ MAHAL

He means it, my lord.

SHAH JAHAN

(Exhausted after the shouting) He does, does he? *(To the* Physician*)* Will you take an oath?

PHYSICIAN

Yes. *(Evasive; moving bottles and bowls)* The cure will work.

SHAH JAHAN

(Lying down) Go on, then. Don't just stand there with that razor in hand.

(The PHYSICIAN *moves.)*

But careful, very careful.

PHYSICIAN

Yes, Your Highness.

(Begins nicking Shah Jahan's *leg.)*

SHAH JAHAN

Not so many cuts, not so deep. Not so deep. *(To* Mumtaz Mahal*)* Where's my astrologer? How much longer will my suffering — Ah! the sting! Ah! Another! Like needles going through. Oh Allah, for what sins am I being punished? *(Moans)* Look, that one! *(Indicates a leech)* Bursting with blood.

(The PHYSICIAN *picks up a fallen leech, and ejects blood from it.)*

Look at all the blood! Royal blood! *(Covers his face with his hands)* I can't bear it. I can't. *(To* Mumtaz Mahal*)* Where's my astrologer? *(Moaning)* When will my fate change? I've done everything — visited all the shrines he suggested, given alms to the needy, and —

MUMTAZ MAHAL

Giving alms is not as effective as shrewd planning, my lord.

SHAH JAHAN

It's too late. I should have done that a long time ago; only I had too much faith in my righteousness. Now it's too late.

MUMTAZ MAHAL
(Enigmatic) For the ingenious it's never too late.

SHAH JAHAN
That's some consolation. *(To the Physician)* How much longer, you blood-sucker?

PHYSICIAN
A bit longer — until the leeches are full.

SHAH JAHAN
Not a moment more. Enough. *(Shakes his legs. Some leeches fall off)* I've had enough.

PHYSICIAN
As Your Highness wishes.
(He puts the leeches away, then picks up the bowl containing blood.)

SHAH JAHAN
No, leave that bowl here.

PHYSICIAN
Yes, Your Highness. *(Puts the vessel down. To Mumtaz Mahal)* His Highness needs a long rest now.

SHAH JAHAN
Rest? I should be preparing to fight Parwez; or at least preparing to take flight. Rest?

MUMTAZ MAHAL
Nowadays Parwez is too drunk to walk, much less march, my lord. He's still celebrating his last victory over us.
(MUMTAZ MAHAL and the PHYSICIAN help SHAH JAHAN to lie down. Stage darkens. The PHYSICIAN pours blood in a bottle. MUMTAZ MAHAL is about to close a window when she sees the PHYSICIAN pouring blood, and stops. Their glances meet. The PHYSICIAN stops, then pours the blood back into the bowl. MUMTAZ MAHAL signals the PHYSICIAN who approaches her up-stage.)

MUMTAZ MAHAL
(Whispering fiercely) So you do sell blood.

PHYSICIAN
(Nervous) I have a large family to support, Your Highness. And I haven't been paid in a long time.

MUMTAZ MAHAL

Nor have others. *(Hotly)* To resort to stealing. And that too
royal blood. You know the punishment for it, don't you?

PHYSICIAN

Please, please, pity my family. Your Highness! I seek
forgiveness.

MUMTAZ MAHAL

Which will not be given, unless — *(Struck with an idea)*
Come here.
(As the PHYSICIAN *approaches her nervously she picks up
a robe.)*
Get into this.

PHYSICIAN

(Taking the robe) I...

MUMTAZ MAHAL

Quick. Over your clothes.
(The PHYSICIAN *obeys.)*
(Examinig him) So I thought. *(Giving him a necklace)* Put
this on.
(The PHYSICIAN *does so.)*
Ah, you are a noble. You are the first Noble of Panigadh on
your way to the camp of Parwez, to join his drunken herd.

PHYSICIAN

(Surprised) Your Highness? *(Alarmed)* Me, in Parwez's
camp? No, please. I'm much too well known.

MUMTAZ MAHAL

As a physician, not as a noble.

PHYSICIAN

Does that make me the real owner of the robe?

MUMTAZ MAHAL

Of course, and of the necklace too. But *(conspiratorially)* at
heart you are still a physician, with knowledge of powders
and potions and herbs that cure — that can cure or kill.

PHYSICIAN

Kill? I'm not used to —

MUMTAZ MAHAL

Aren't you? Aren't you used to administering powders and potions to sick people — such as Parwez? Haven't you heard of Parwez's chronic constipation?

PHYSICIAN

(Receptive) I have.

MUMTAZ MAHAL

Won't you cure him, then? A permanent cure? Won't you? For a permanent title later, when justice has won over intrigue. Won't you fight for justice with your means?

PHYSICIAN

I think, I might... I will.

(Intermittent mumbling by SHAH JAHAN in his sleep.)

MUMTAZ MAHAL

Make haste then. Take the fastest horse, and some gold coins.

(She gives him a bag of coins.)

PHYSICIAN

Gold! Your Highness is most generous.

MUMTAZ MAHAL

I wish you success.

(The PHYSICIAN leaves.)

MUMTAZ MAHAL

Some fight clean, others not —

SHAH JAHAN

The horses! The horses are coming! *(Gets up)* The horses galloping. Parwez! It's Parwez!

MUMTAZ MAHAL

(Caressing him) I heard nothing. *(Goes to the window)* I see nothing.

SHAH JAHAN

(Lost) Was I dreaming then?

MUMTAZ MAHAL

Perhaps.

SHAH JAHAN

(Sadly) What dreams! I used to dream of a city of my own, Shah Jahan Abad, with a fort and gardens, and palaces and bazaars — but no longer. Once I was the most

favourite prince; now I'm branded 'Wretch of the Moghul Empire'. *(To* Mumtaz Mahal*)* Whatever has happened to my astrologer?

MUMTAZ MAHAL
(Haltingly) There's no trace of him.

SHAH JAHAN
Disappeared? Has he? He may have. Out of fear for being wrong so often. *(Brief pause)* He was a bad astrologer, really: he couldn't make up his mind whether Allah or man was the maker of man's fate.

MUMTAZ MAHAL
(Crisply) It is man.

SHAH JAHAN
You sound emphatic, the way I used to. I used to believe that Allah rewarded good over evil, but I'm no longer sure. Now, I'm like the old astrologer. *(Pause)* Not really, for he was never short of optimism, whereas mine is running out.

MUMTAZ MAHAL
Please don't despair, my lord.

SHAH JAHAN
Despair is all I have.

MUMTAZ MAHAL
But you needn't; because the future is likely to favour us.

SHAH JAHAN
(Puzzled, yet interested) How?

MUMTAZ MAHAL
If Shahriyar gets the throne, Parwez will be angered, and will join us to right the wrong. If and when Parwez gets it, he'll not live long to enjoy it, being a slave to drink, not to mention his chronic constipation.

SHAH JAHAN
Ah, his chronic constipation! *(Chuckles)* Mine is just a passing ailment, but his chronic... *(chuckles)*... What logic flows from your sweet lips! You represent a perfect blending of beauty and reason. You are better than all the physicians put together.

MUMTAZ MAHAL

I'm no more than an admirer of my lord.

SHAH JAHAN

More, much more. You are my wife, my beloved, my companion in play. Come, let's have a game of chess. Let me excercise my mind.

MUMTAZ MAHAL

Hadn't we better...

(Enter a STRANGER struggling with the EUNUCH. MUMTAZ MAHAL steps back.)

SHAH JAHAN

(After the initial surprise) Stop it!

EUNUCH

This scoundrel, Your Highness! I tried to stop him. He refuses to identify himself.

STRANGER

(With a deep bow) He wanted me to bribe him, Your Highness. I refused — being a messenger of Prime Minister Asaf Khan with a most urgent...

SHAH JAHAN

(Impatient) Then say it, you fool.

STRANGER

Emperor Jahangir is dead.

SHAH JAHAN

(With mixed feelings) Dead? *Ina la lilahe wu ina ilahe rajoon!‡ (To the* Stranger*)* How did he die? Where?

STRANGER

In Kashmir, while travelling to Agra. The Emperor was weak, very weak. But His Majesty wanted to hunt. So they had a herd of deer ready to cross a gorge, as His Majesty stood at the pass with a loaded gun. Suddenly, a helper fell off a precipice and perished under his eyes. The sight unhinged the Emperor who died the same night.

---

‡ A Quranic verse which a Muslim should recite in honour of the dead. It means: 'We are from Allah, and we return to Allah'.

SHAH JAHAN

May his soul rest in paradise! *(Pause)* So the imperial throne lies vacant.

STRANGER

(Hesitant) Prince Shahriyar... he sits on it... *(Firmly)* But he was not named by the Emperor; no one was named by the Emperor.

MUMTAZ MAHAL

(Anxious) And my father?

STRANGER

He's still the Prime Minister. He sent me by two of his fastest horses. *(To* Shah Jahan*)* He wishes to advise Your Highness to start marching northward, now, to prove false the news of your ill health.

SHAH JAHAN

(Excited) Whose ill health? *(Getting up)* I'm hale and hearty: I'm in excellent health.

STRANGER

It's the rumours, Your Highness. Rumours travel faster than the wind. I had hardly crossed the river Jamuna when I heard that Prince Shahriyar was sending emissaries to Your Highness's camp.

MUMTAZ MAHAL

(Alarmed) What for?

STRANGER

I didn't ask. I was in a hurry to get here.

MUMTAZ MAHAL

And Parwez? Does he know about the Emperor?

STRANGER

The Prime Minister sent him no urgent message.

MUMTAZ MAHAL

(Brooding) What could Shahriyar's emissaries want?

SHAH JAHAN

Don't worry. Let me have my robes of mourning.
(Enter the PHYSICIAN *straggling like drunk.)*

PHYSICIAN

Wines, delicious wines...*(Noticing* Mumtaz Mahal*)* The powder worked... the powder worked well... *(chuckles)* so well... his bowels loosened... he went on... and on and on... *(farts)*... on and on until he fell... unconscious... he didn't wake... *(He looks at* Mumtaz Mahal *and takes off his necklace)* Fake...

MUMTAZ MAHAL

(Angered) Shut up!

SHAH JAHAN

(Puzzled) What's he mumbling about. *(To* Mumtaz Mahal*)* Whose death? And who's he? It seems he's wearing a robe of mine. How did he get here?

MUMTAZ MAHAL

We'll know when he sobers up - if he does. *(To the* Eunuch *and the* Stranger*)* Take him away.
(The EUNUCH *and the* STRANGER *starts dragging the* Physician.*)*

SHAH JAHAN

(Irritated) Quiet! I hear something. Like a mob collecting for a wrestling match. At this hour? *(To the* Eunuch*)* Find out.

EUNUCH

Yes, Your Highness.
(He leaves.)

MUMTAZ MAHAL

(To the Stranger*)* You stay at the entrance.

STRANGER

Yes, Your Highness.
(He leaves.)

SHAH JAHAN

(Excited) I wish my astrologer were here to witness this. The imperial throne is at last mine.

MUMTAZ MAHAL

Not quite, my lord. Something tells me — not quite yet.

SHAH JAHAN

(Puzzled) What could go wrong?

MUMTAZ MAHAL

The last step on the ladder can be the most slippery. So, please, be careful.
(Enter the EUNUCH.*)*

MUMTAZ MAHAL

What did you find?

EUNUCH

Emissaries from the court of Emperor Shahriyar have come. Two —

SHAH JAHAN

(Furious) Em-per-or Shahriyar?

MUMTAZ MAHAL

Why were they mobbed?

EUNUCH

There's suspicion that they have a strong army to support them. Only a few miles from our camp.

SHAH JAHAN

(Derisive) Rumours!

MUMTAZ MAHAL

Tell them my lord is very ill.

EUNUCH

I did. And they said that they had an important message for the prince if he were sick.

MUMTAZ MAHAL

(Troubled) If? Why if? *(To the* Eunuch; *firmly)* Tell them to wait — until the whistle blows.

EUNUCH

Yes, Your Highness.
*(*SHAH JAHAN, *fidgeting with the whistle, prepares to speak when –)*

PHYSICIAN

(From behind the screen) Soldiers... march... on ... and on...
(sings) round and round... on and on...

SHAH JAHAN

Shut up! *(To* Mumtaz Mahal*)* Where are my mourning robes?

MUMTAZ MAHAL

Hadn't we better wait for the news to come officially, from the emissaries? *(Appealing)* Please, let us act weak and ill-informed. Let us lull Shahriyar into complacency by lying low.

SHAH JAHAN

Lie low while the imperial throne awaits me?

MUMTAZ MAHAL

(Sharply) What probably awaits you now is the army of Shahriyar. All around the camp.

SHAH JAHAN

The dark period of our life is over, yet you can't see a rope without calling it a snake. Look up! And face the light!

MUMTAZ MAHAL

No, no. I'm convinced this is a false ray of hope. Please take my advice: lie low, act ill, dangerously ill. Not just act. Be dangerously ill. *(Wrings her hands)* How? The Physician. He'd know.
(She goes behind the curtain, kicks the Physician.*)*
Wake up! *(The* PHYSICIAN *grunts)* It's hopeless.

SHAH JAHAN

Oh, please — *(Sits down.)*

MUMTAZ MAHAL

(Caught up in her thought) There must be a way. There's got to be. *(In the course of nervous pacing she stumbles against a bowl)* Oh, the bowls and bottles! *(While putting the bowl away, she notices a bottle full of blood)* Blood. Yes. That should do. *(About to spill blood on the floor, when –)* No. Something spontaneous. Genuine. *(To* Shah Jahan*)* Please — just drink it.

SHAH JAHAN

(Stunned) What!

MUMTAZ MAHAL

Please drink this.

SHAH JAHAN

Drink blood! My own blood? Are you out of your senses?

MUMTAZ MAHAL

On the contrary. Nothing stimulates my mind better than a crisis. And we're in the middle of one. Please do as I suggest.

SHAH JAHAN

Oh, let things be! Don't force events.

MUMTAZ MAHAL

If you don't, the events may force you — and us all— right out of existence. Can't you see we are trapped, surrounded? We have to contrive to get out alive.

SHAH JAHAN

(Amenable) How will my drinking blood get us out?

MUMTAZ MAHAL

This is how.
(She whispers to him.)

SHAH JAHAN

It won't work.

MUMTAZ MAHAL

Leave it to me.

SHAH JAHAN

Supposing it fails to work.

MUMTAZ MAHAL

There's no time to speculate. Please. *(Appealing)* Please do this for me.

SHAH JAHAN

All right, I will, this time. Never again. *(Grabs the bottle)* Oh, to be forced to drink strange liquids: first wine, now this — *(Takes long gulps. Lies down.)*

MUMTAZ MAHAL

Now!
(She blows the whistle. The EUNUCH *enters.)*

EUNUCH

The emissaries of His Majesty Emperor Shahriyar!

FIRST EMISSARY

(Entering) I bring greeting from —
(He stops in horror as Shah Jahan's *bloody vomit spatters his dress. The next vomit falls on the floor.)*

MUMTAZ MAHAL

The condition of my lord is very grave.

FIRST EMISSARY

(Still shaken) Yes, we see it. We came to convey the order of Emperor Shahriyar that Prince Shah Jahan is to remain here.

MUMTAZ MAHAL

Where else can he go — in this state?

SECOND EMISSARY

We realise it now, and convey our deepest sympathies.

MUMTAZ MAHAL

(Performing a painful duty) Should the inevitable happen, should the call of Allah become urgent, then the body of my lord can't wait here. It's the dynastic tradition that the royal princes be buried in the capital.

SECOND EMISSARY

Yes, the tradition is widely known. We don't see any objection being raised by the Royal Council to the burial in Agra.

FIRST EMISSARY

Side by side with Prince Parwez, perhaps.

MUMTAZ MAHAL

No!

FIRST EMISSARY

(Blandly) We saw the hearse ourselves. They say he died of an excessive dose of laxatives.

MUMTAZ MAHAL

Please don't shout the news. It'll grieve my lord. Prince Parwez was, after all, his blood brother.

SECOND EMISSARY

Now we must leave.

(As the EMISSARIES prepare to leave, SHAH JAHAN vomits noisily. Brief silence. Back-stage goes dark. Then wails of MUMTAZ MAHAL.)

FIRST EMISSARY

May his soul rest in paradise! *Ina la lilahe wu ina ilahe rajoon!*

SECOND EMISSARY

No use leaving the imperial forces circling his camp now.

FIRST EMISSARY

No; none at all.

ACT THREE
Scene 1

A year later. Evening. A courtyard where MUMTAZ
MAHAL *sits on a swing while a* MAID *plaits her hair.
Another* MAID, *squatting on a carpet, plays a lute. Next to
her is a large bowl of ice covered with sawdust. There is an
air of festivity.*

FIRST MAID
(Singing) After the rains, air is cool, cool... After the rains,
air is cool, cool, cool...
MUMTAZ MAHAL
You have been singing that all afternoon.
FIRST MAID
It has such a soothing effect, Your Majesty.
MUMTAZ MAHAL
It isn't the song, you fool; it's the block of ice you are sitting
next to.
FIRST MAID
(Jerking her body) Ooo! *(Childishly inquisitive)* Is ice cold,
Your Majesty?
MUMTAZ MAHAL
(Imperially) Of course.
FIRST MAID
I've never seen ice before. Where does it grow?
MUMTAZ MAHAL
(Curtly) Your Majesty.
FIRST MAID
(Crushed) Your Majesty. Where does ice grow?
MUMTAZ MAHAL
It forms on top of mountains.
FIRST MAID
(Puzzled) Falls?
MUMTAZ MAHAL
Forms, not falls, you fool. Forms from snow which falls
from the sky.

FIRST MAID

Oh! *(After-thought)* Your Majesty.

MUMTAZ MAHAL

Get me a piece.

FIRST MAID

(Rises) Yes, Your Majesty.
(She breaks a piece, washes it, and takes it to Mumtaz Mahal.*)*

MUMTAZ MAHAL

Ah, so cold. Refreshing! *(Rubbing it over her cheeks, then lips)* I often wonder why my forefathers left the cool heights of Samarkand. Was it the urge to conquer the plains and rule? *(Firmly)* To rule.
(She rubs the piece over her forehead, then puts it in her mouth. Holding up a mirror in her hand.)
Mumps; I've mumps.
(She bursts out laughing. The ice flies off her mouth and hits the mirror.)
Oh! I can't see... *(To the* Maids*)* Clean it.
(The FIRST MAID *takes the mirror and rubs it with her scarf.)*
Not with that, you fool. Haven't I told you to use only the silk scarves? Venetian silks.

FIRST MAID

(Stupidly) Venetian?

MUMTAZ MAHAL

Yes, from Venice, across the seven seas. Haven't you seen the bundles lying around?

FIRST MAID

(Nervous) No; yes. I'll get one, Your Majesty.
(She exits.)

MUMTAZ MAHAL

When will she realise she's a maid to the Empress of Hindostan?

SECOND MAID

She's slow in her wits, Your Majesty.

MUMTAZ MAHAL

(Haughtily) And I am short of patience.

SECOND MAID

The change is a bit too much for her young mind, Your Majesty. All these festivities of the coronation: the daily processions, the fireworks, the feasts. She had never tasted so many fruits and meats and sweets before as she did last night and the night before and the —

MUMTAZ MAHAL

(Sharply) And you?

SECOND MAID

(Recovering quickly from a surprise) Never. Never before had I seen so many fruits and sweets, Your Majesty, much less eaten them. *(Effusive)* They say never before has this dynasty seen such festivities.

MUMTAZ MAHAL

(Part-defensively) It's all within the edicts of Islam: not a drop of wine anywhere. And everywhere in the capital, alms for the needy, clothes for the naked, dowries for the daughters of the poor.

SECOND MAID

May Allah be merciful! May Allah give us a long and just rule of His Majesty!

MUMTAZ MAHAL

(Confidently) He will. He will. *(Caressing her hair)* Is my hair growing?

SECOND MAID

Yes, Your Majesty. *(Measuring it)* It's an elbow and four fingers long. Last week it was an elbow and two fingers. It's a sign of good health.

MUMTAZ MAHAL

I want it even longer.

SECOND MAID

I'll make it so with these braids.
(She bows to pick up the braids and notices SHAH JAHAN, with a rose in hand, entering quietly. SHAH JAHAN signals her to leave. She leaves. SHAH JAHAN tiptoes towards Mumtaz Mahal and starts to fix braids to her hair.)

MUMTAZ MAHAL

Not so hard. Don't pull my hair out.

SHAH JAHAN

(In a feigned female voice) Beg pardon, Your Majesty.

MUMTAZ MAHAL

What's happened to your voice?

SHAH JAHAN

Nothing, Your Majesty.

(He fixes a rose to her hair.)

MUMTAZ MAHAL

Don't poke my head.

(She pulls her hair and finds a rose. Surprised, she turns around and discovers Shah Jahan.)

(Mimicking) Nothing, Your Majesty. You can't plait hair.

SHAH JAHAN

You can let me try.

MUMTAZ MAHAL

If you wish.

SHAH JAHAN

My wishes and your genius.

MUMTAZ MAHAL

(Half seriously and half jokingly) Where's my reward?

SHAH JAHAN

For what?

MUMTAZ MAHAL

My genius.

SHAH JAHAN

Oh? Your genius. *(Kneeling)* Here it is: yours.

(MUMTAZ MAHAL bends forward and kisses his forehead. SHAH JAHAN rises to his feet, sits on the swing. They laugh as SHAH JAHAN sets the swing in motion.)

MUMTAZ MAHAL

My lord.

SHAH JAHAN

Yes.

MUMTAZ MAHAL

(Seriously) What have you decided about Rodreguiz and his Christians?

SHAH JAHAN

(Off-handed) What more is there to decide? I have been chasing the poor wretches to the far corners of the Empire. I've banished their priest from the court and destroyed their paintings. That should be enough.

MUMTAZ MAHAL

Not as far as I'm concerned.

SHAH JAHAN

I don't want to waste any more money on them. I'd rather spend it on buildings; on the gardens here, and the plans for a new city.

(MUMTAZ MAHAL snaps herself free and sets the swing in motion.)

What's the matter? What —

(He tries to stop the swing, fails; tries again, succeeds.)

Please. What's come over you?

MUMTAZ MAHAL

They abducted my maids when I needed them most. I swallowed that humiliation then. But now, when I can avenge it in full, you compromise.

SHAH JAHAN

All right. I'll send a large force against them — tomorrow with special instructions to catch Rodreguiz. Does that please you enough *(holding up her chin)* to give me a smile? *(MUMTAZ MAHAL smiles)* That's better, much better... Be happy. It's still the coronation month.

(Sounds of fireworks, off-stage.)

They can't wait; the sun is hardly down. Come.

MUMTAZ MAHAL

Look, that rocket! It glows only for a moment. But while it does, it lights up the whole sky.

SHAH JAHAN

Come to the balcony. We'll be able to see better.

MUMTAZ MAHAL

Let me get my veil.

SHAH JAHAN

No one will notice.

MUMTAZ MAHAL

(Brooding) To be all powerful, yet unknown. *(To* Shah Jahan*)* Will you play chess with me afterwards?

SHAH JAHAN

Not tonight. Not this week.

(They exit.)

Scene 2

Two years later. Afternoon. The Royal tower, Agra, without the Christian paintings and wine jars. Wooden steps in the left hand corner lead to an object covered with a sheet. SHAH JAHAN and MUMTAZ MAHAL sit on a mattressed dais facing each other over a large chess-board. They have just finished a game. She is rearranging the pieces, while he draws on his hooka.

SHAH JAHAN

If only I hadn't played the elephant. Anyway, the next game will be mine.

MUMTAZ MAHAL

(Stretching herself) Let's stop now. I feel tired.

SHAH JAHAN

One more game won't tire you. Just one.

MUMTAZ MAHAL

It gets rather dull when I keep winning every time.

SHAH JAHAN

That's because I don't take it seriously.

MUMTAZ MAHAL

Why don't you?

SHAH JAHAN

I can't treat you as a rival; you are my wife.

MUMTAZ MAHAL

That's no reason to deprive me of the excitement of competition.

SHAH JAHAN

I'll make the next game exciting. *(Smoking)* I hope luck is with me this time.

MUMTAZ MAHAL

(Firmly) It's not luck; it's the capacity of one's mind to be able to see far ahead.

SHAH JAHAN

No. It's luck, more or less; and I've been out of it for sometime. *(Smoking)* But it'll change: the next game'll be mine.

MUMTAZ MAHAL

You sound certain.

SHAH JAHAN

Very.

MUMTAZ MAHAL

Will you stake something then?

SHAH JAHAN

This is just a game.

MUMTAZ MAHAL

If you continue treating this as just a game, you'll never win. You should play for stakes.

SHAH JAHAN

(Amenable) Like?

MUMTAZ MAHAL

Like... something important... valuable.

SHAH JAHAN

Rubies?

MUMTAZ MAHAL

I have so many already.

SHAH JAHAN

Diamonds, then?

MUMTAZ MAHAL

The same thing: even Court nobles have them.

SHAH JAHAN

(Stung) What do you mean even Court nobles?

MUMTAZ MAHAL

Well, I'd prefer something... truly royal.

SHAH JAHAN

The Crown jewels, for example. *(Quietly sarcastic)* Or, perhaps, the Crown itself.

MUMTAZ MAHAL

(Blandly) No, the Crown lands will do. I'll stake the lands you gave me on the eve of your coronation.

SHAH JAHAN

So that if you lose them now, I should give them back to you on your next birthday. *(Chuckling)* How very bold.

MUMTAZ MAHAL

(Incensed) I won't lose the lands if you lose the game, will I? It'll be you who will have to match my stake.

SHAH JAHAN

(Serious) I'll more than match it. I'll double it, treble it.

MUMTAZ MAHAL

I'll match yours by adding all my private gold and silver.

SHAH JAHAN

How high can you go?

MUMTAZ MAHAL

As high as you'll take it.

SHAH JAHAN

You don't really mean it.

MUMTAZ MAHAL

I do.

SHAH JAHAN

(Dead serious) Could you match my throne?

MUMTAZ MAHAL

(Disbelieving) Your throne? *(Coming down)* Of course, I couldn't. Nobody could. *(Brief pause)* It'd be no use to me even if won it. I can't sit on it.

SHAH JAHAN

(Still tense) Who said so?

MUMTAZ MAHAL

The edicts of the Holy Quran: they forbid a woman from exposing herself to male strangers.

SHAH JAHAN

There are no strangers in here, male or female.

MUMTAZ MAHAL

In this chamber, you mean.

SHAH JAHAN

Yes, but that's immaterial — for the next game will be mine.

MUMTAZ MAHAL

Let's play and find out. *(She arranges the rest of the pieces.)*

SHAH JAHAN

No, I want the black, lucky black.
(They turn the board around.)

SHAH JAHAN

Your move.

MUMTAZ MAHAL

No, yours. I won the last game.

SHAH JAHAN

All right. *(Hastily)* Here.
(He moves.)

MUMTAZ MAHAL

Hmm... *(Deliberately)* Well. *(Moves.)*
(They make a few moves each.)

SHAH JAHAN

Nothing clever.
(He moves hastily.)

MUMTAZ MAHAL

Quite simple to block that. But I'd rather... *(Moves.)*

SHAH JAHAN

(Jubilant) How easily you fell into my trap. *(Moving hastily)* Here.
(Pause, while MUMTAZ MAHAL *studies the situation.)*
(Triumphant) Trapped.

MUMTAZ MAHAL

I think I'll play the queen.
(She moves.)

SHAH JAHAN

A colossal risk, doing that, at this stage of the game. I play the horse.
(He moves.)

MUMTAZ MAHAL

(Slowly) There. *(Moving)* Check your king.

SHAH JAHAN

(Surprised) Really?

MUMTAZ MAHAL

Yes.

SHAH JAHAN

I can easily save it. *(Moving, then retrieving)* No. *(Moving again)* There.

MUMTAZ MAHAL

Not really. *(Moving)* Check.

SHAH JAHAN

No! *(Pause)* I'll get out, you'll see. *(Making a tentative move)* No, this won't do. *(Another move)* Yes.

MUMTAZ MAHAL

(Moving quietly) Checkmate.

SHAH JAHAN

(Nervous) This can't be. *(Pause)* There must be a way out.

MUMTAZ MAHAL

Find it.

SHAH JAHAN

How can I? With all this distraction? *(Making a few desperate moves)* No. It's hopeless. Well...

MUMTAZ MAHAL

So you lose?

SHAH JAHAN

I... I suppose so.

MUMTAZ MAHAL

Where's the throne?

SHAH JAHAN

What throne?

MUMTAZ MAHAL

The one you staked.

SHAH JAHAN

Oh, this one. Yes. *(He gets up)* Here.

MUMTAZ MAHAL

I don't see it.

SHAH JAHAN

(Moving up to the steps) Under the sheet. *(He lifts the sheet to reveal a gilted throne.)*

MUMTAZ MAHAL

Ah, the new throne; but it doesn't look real.

SHAH JAHAN

It's a model, though the colour is true. And even the real throne couldn't possibly be more comfortable. *(Feeling the seat)* All pigeon feathers.

MUMTAZ MAHAL

It was supposed to be flanked by peacocks, you once told me.

SHAH JAHAN

It was — until I came across this book compiled by my father in the library, with the sketches of all the birds in the Empire: silver doves, scarlet macaws, green parakeets, pink parrots, white pelicans, hundreds of them. Under each sketch were written the habits of the birds — what it ate, how high it flew and so on. I discovered that the eagle flies the highest. Ugly bird but *(caressing the eagles flanking the throne)* it flies with the clouds.

MUMTAZ MAHAL

The throne doesn't have to fly.

SHAH JAHAN

I wish it did. *(Caressing the birds)* I wish these were real birds with strong wings powerful enough to carry the throne to the skies. I'd love that feeling: free as air, light as a feather. This morning when I sat on it I felt dizzy, the way I used to when riding elephants. I could feel my mind crowding with poetry.

MUMTAZ MAHAL

(Eagerly) Will mine?

SHAH JAHAN

Discover it for yourself.

MUMTAZ MAHAL

Then let me.

SHAH JAHAN

Yes.

(He comes down the steps.)

(Extends his hands) Come.

(MUMTAZ MAHAL *gets up. She places one hand on her pregnant belly and gives the other to* Shah Jahan. *Then suddenly –)*

MUMTAZ MAHAL

(Withdrawing her hands) No.

SHAH JAHAN

(Surprised) No?

MUMTAZ MAHAL

I can't... I... I feel afraid. The height...

SHAH JAHAN

There's nothing to fear, my Mumtaz. *(Tightening his grip)* I'll lead you up. It's only a game.

MUMTAZ MAHAL

(Puzzled) I thought this was real.

SHAH JAHAN

Imagine it to be a game.

MUMTAZ MAHAL

Hm...

SHAH JAHAN

Come.

(MUMTAZ MAHAL follows SHAH JAHAN *up the steps. She stumbles.)*

Careful!

(At the top of the steps) The royal throne... at your feet. But — wait. Let me announce you!

MUMTAZ MAHAL

If you so wish.

(SHAH JAHAN steps down.)

SHAH JAHAN

The Empress of Hindostan, the Light of the World, the Defender of the Faith, Her Majesty Mumtaz Mahal Begum!

MUMTAZ MAHAL

(Sitting down) There's no one around to hear it.

SHAH JAHAN

(Enthusiastic) Then we'll imagine it... so vividly that it will become more real than the reality. *(Pompously)* On the tier directly below Your Majesty's throne stand the royal princes, dignified and graceful, yet subdued and respectful. On the tier below that, stand the ambassadors from foreign lands; and below them the court nobles, each one dressed more ornately than the other, hands on the swords, and *(indicating)* over there, beyond the forecourt, in the sun, stand the subjects, hoping for a glimpse of the Empress, a glimpse they'll always be denied. *(Softly)* Imagine all that.

MUMTAZ MAHAL

(Sulking) You do that.

SHAH JAHAN

You too should try. Imagination is important; for fact flows from fancy. And fancy can be more powerful than facts, sometimes. It was my fancy that fed my emaciated soul through the darkest days of my life.

MUMTAZ MAHAL

(Irritated) Your fancy. And where was I?

SHAH JAHAN

(Surprised) You?

MUMTAZ MAHAL

Yes, me.

SHAH JAHAN

Of course dearest, you were important — too.

MUMTAZ MAHAL

Just that? I thought I was very very important to you, crucially important.

SHAH JAHAN

What was crucially important was my confidence in my future, in the ultimate victory of justice over intrigue.

MUMTAZ MAHAL

Where did that confidence of yours take you? Into a sick bed beseiged by the forces of Shahriyar.

SHAH JAHAN

That was a stroke of bad luck.

MUMTAZ MAHAL

Bad luck? Or, a series of bad moves — as in your game of chess — like your reluctance to hire Christians to fight Parwez?

SHAH JAHAN

(Gravely) Religious principles were involved. Did you expect me to discard them as easily as Rodreguiz did his Christian robes?

MUMTAZ MAHAL

(Hotly) Principles, principles. What good are principles if they restrict one's ability to manoeuvre, hasten one's downfall? How can one uphold them when one is powerless — or non-existent, like Parwez. He too had principles, so he claimed; and now earthworms fatten themselves on him. *(Pause)* Have you ever wondered about his death?

SHAH JAHAN

No. *(Brief pause)* What's there to wonder about? He was a drunk, obsessed with stiff bowels; and he died of an overdose of laxatives.

MUMTAZ MAHAL

At a very convenient time too — soon after the Emperor's death.

SHAH JAHAN

I don't see the connection. *(Exasperated)* Why are you raking up the past, anyway? I don't understand.

MUMTAZ MAHAL

You would, if you understood intrigue.

SHAH JAHAN

I don't. *(Hotly)* And what's more, I won't.

MUMTAZ MAHAL

Then you will end up losing what you now hold.

SHAH JAHAN

Is that a threat or a prophecy?

MUMTAZ MAHAL

(Belittling the question) Me, your most beloved wife, threatening? You're getting far too sensitive. Or have I really touched a raw nerve? *(Pause)* You are perhaps not as

innocent as you are trying to appear. There's probably some intrigue you do understand.

SHAH JAHAN

(Begrudging) If my vomiting blood is to be termed intrigue, yes.

MUMTAZ MAHAL

(Derisive) No, I'm not thinking of that. That was a defensive act. *(Solemnly)* I'm thinking of active, positive intrigue. *(Brief pause)* Remember what my father did when your hearse neared Agra?

SHAH JAHAN

Ah, yes. *(Recalling with relish)* That was clever, supremely clever — fooling Shahriyar by reminding him of the convention that my hearse had to be received with full regal honours, outside the city gates. What a clever way to empty the Royal Fort of all its cavalry! *(Chuckling)* Shariyar was too gullible. He shouldn't have believed the news of my death: he should have been sceptical.

MUMTAZ MAHAL

(Abrasively) Were you sceptical?

SHAH JAHAN

(Irritated) Of what?

MUMTAZ MAHAL

The reports of chaos in the province of Parwez when you were marching southward.

SHAH JAHAN

I don't remember.
(He walks towards his hooka.)

MUMTAZ MAHAL

(With a sardonic smile) Don't remember — or conveniently forget. *(No response)* Well, at least, you're learning.

SHAH JAHAN

So, you approve of my lying.

MUMTAZ MAHAL

I approve or disapprove of something only within the circumstances. Lying is neither good nor bad in itself.

SHAH JAHAN

(Picking up his hooka) Novel, very novel. Suddenly you're brimming with original ideas.

MUMTAZ MAHAL

I've always brimmed with original ideas.

SHAH JAHAN

Was it modesty, then, which kept them locked in?

MUMTAZ MHAHAL

It was more a sense of timing. When one is beleaguered by adversaries, fighting for one's life, one should worry less about self-expression and more about self-preservation. It's different now; only you and me left. In life timing is crucial.

SHAH JAHAN

(Half deprecating) Yes, very much so.
(He sits down, smokes hooka.)
What was that you said, only you and me left?

MUMTAZ MAHAL

(With quiet firmness) Stand up and talk.

SHAH JAHAN

(Surprised but calm) Why?

MUMTAZ MAHAL

Not why, stand up.

SHAH JAHAN

(Subdued) You can't...

MUMTAZ MAHAL

(Solemnly) No one sits in the presence of the Empress.

SHAH JAHAN

This is just a game, Mumtaz.

MUMTAZ MAHAL

Use the title.

SHAH JAHAN

(Subdued) Yes, Your —

MUMTAZ MAHAL

(Impatient) Majesty.

SHAH JAHAN

(Bowing) Your Majesty, this is just a game.

MUMTAZ MAHAL

Imagine it to be real. Imagine.

SHAH JAHAN

(Lost) Imagine?

MUMTAZ MAHAL

Yes, your favourite word, your repeated advice to others. Now you imagine.

SHAH JAHAN

(Still lost) Imagine... what?

MUMTAZ MAHAL

That I'm the Empress, and I sit on the imperial throne.

SHAH JAHAN

(Weakly) This is only a model.

MUMTAZ MAHAL

No; this is real: an ideal throne, made of gold. Touch it, feel it. I sit on it; and I have the power to do anything I choose... anything... even order you about. Why just order? I may even punish you.

SHAH JAHAN

(Aghast) For what? My own wife, threatening to punish me? What's come over you? You're under a spell; you've been possessed by the Satan himself.

MUMTAZ MAHAL

(Sharply) And you by moral arrogance — for too long. Time and again you looked the other way while others intrigued for you, so that you could proclaim at the top of your voice that you were morally impeccable. Now you smugly enjoy the fruits of their efforts, oblivious of the pangs of their consciences.

SHAH JAHAN

Whose consciences?

MUMTAZ MAHAL

My father's, for having Shahriyar thrown into a well. *(Afterthought)* And mine, too.

SHAH JAHAN

Yours?

MUMTAZ MAHAL

For what I did to Parwez.

SHAH JAHAN

What could you have done to him: you hardly knew him.

MUMTAZ MAHAL

That didn't stop me from having him poisoned.

SHAH JAHAN

Poisoned? *(Unbelieving)* You had him poisoned? You didn't. *(Half deprecating)* You couldn't even if you wanted to. That's just not true.

MUMTAZ MAHAL

It's as true as the pock-marks under your beard.

SHAH JAHAN

All right, suppose you did have him poisoned. So what? I can't be expected to share the responsibility. It was entirely your idea.

MUMTAZ MAHAL

Which stemmed directly from my love for you, and was meant to get you what you so keenly desired.

SHAH JAHAN

Let's not confuse means with ends.

MUMTAZ MAHAL

They're inseparable, like day and night: so you've declared time and again. Today, I'll judge you by *your* standards, *your* values.

SHAH JAHAN

Please, this is just a game.

MUMTAZ MAHAL

With very high stakes. And you've lost. I'm ready to announce the verdict. Give me the whistle. I want the Prime Minister called.

SHAH JAHAN

That won't help. He's much too loyal to me.

MUMTAZ MAHAL

Not as much as he's to me. You'll see.

SHAH JAHAN

(Exasperated) This is ludicrous.

MUMTAZ MAHAL

The Royal Court demands restraint and respect. There are princes and ambasssdors present.

SHAH JAHAN

(Hotly) There is no one present.

MUMTAZ MAHAL

How then did you describe them so vividly?

SHAH JAHAN

Oh, that was all imaginary.

MUMTAZ MAHAL

(Curtly) I order that you go on a pilgrimage to Mecca and pray for those who intrigued for you. Or divide the Empire into two, and give the better half to them.

SHAH JAHAN

(Upset) Is this justice? Or more a mockery of it?

MUMTAZ MAHAL

Then you are mocking at your own standards.

SHAH JAHAN

I need time to choose between your alternatives to me.

MUMTAZ MAHAL

You'll have it. But don't leave the Court.

SHAH JAHAN

I won't... Your Majesty.
(He bows, then moves down-stage.)
(Softly) How did I get into this? I must do something — and restore the previous order. No. I can't. It'd be worse, if I failed. *(Wistfully)* I wish someone would come in now. That won't help. Whosoever comes in would probably think me a fool to have let her sit on the throne, or to have lost it in a game of chess. I need time to think. But how am I to get it? Under the guise of a prayer. But I can't pray. I don't have the mat. Doesn't matter. I could pray without it. No one would dare disturb a man in prayer. Yes, I'll out-fox the vixen, give her a dose of her own medicine. I've got to get out of this by fair means or foul.
(As he kneels, he notices ASAF KHAN *entering, then hesitating.)*
No, no, don't leave.

ASAF KHAN
(Re-entering) I did not mean to disturb.
(He notices Mumtaz Mahal.*)*
(Puzzled) She?!

SHAH JAHAN
Not she. Her Majesty.

ASAF KHAN
(Bowing) I beg Your Majesty's pardon.

MUMTAZ MAHAL
Pardon granted. What business brings you here?

ASAF KHAN
Padre Rodreguiz, Your Majesty. He has been brought to the fort as a prisoner.

MUMTAZ MAHAL
Then bring him before me.
(ASAF KHAN bows and leaves.)

MUMTAZ MAHAL
Now it's the padre's turn to pay for his crimes.

SHAH JAHAN
He was only trying to spread his religion.

MUMTAZ MAHAL
You don't have to plead for him. What have you decided for yourself?

SHAH JAHAN
I need more time.
(Enter ASAF KHAN *followed by* RODREGUIZ, *who instantly prostrates himself before* Shah Jahan.*)*

RODREGUIZ
A thousand prostrations, Your Majesty!

SHAH JAHAN
(Sarcastic) At last you're doing the right thing, but to the wrong person. It's the Empress who rules.
(RODREGUIZ rises to his feet and looks at Mumtaz Mahal, *agape.)*

RODREGUIZ
(Lying down) A thousand prostrations, Your Majesty!

MUMTAZ MAHAL

(Haughtily) Prostration is not required: it violates my religion. Bowing will do.

(RODREGUIZ rises to his feet.)

RODREGUIZ

I'm innocent, Your Majesty. I'm a man of religion, not of war.

MUMTAZ MAHAL

The two are joined together, like body and soul.

RODREGUIZ

They probably are, Your Majesty, though not in my case. I make no war.

MUMTAZ MAHAL

(Taunting) No, you just exploit them. You promise support to both sides, and fight for neither. You just leave your colonies at night, and the nearby villagers find their women and cattle missing the next morning.

RODREGUIZ

I never abduct or steal, Your Majesty.

MUMTAZ MAHAL

You just incite others to do so.

RODREGUIZ

(Grudgingly) Sometimes, some of my flock get carried away by their passion for Christianity. I can't control them.

MUMTAZ MAHAL

You don't even try.

RODREGUIZ

In all honesty, I shouldn't; because they think they're serving their religion that way.

MUMTAZ MAHAL

(With contempt) What an ignoble way!

RODREGUIZ

That doesn't matter, for they believe it's for a noble end. More women in our Christian colonies means more Christians.

MUMTAZ MAHAL

(Indicating Shah Jahan) Tell him that.

SHAH JAHAN

(Grumpy) I heard; noble end through ignoble means.

MUMTAZ MAHAL

(To Shah Jahan*)* Would you *still* plead for him?

SHAH JAHAN

I never wanted to, Your Majesty.

RODREGUIZ

(With feigned surprise) Plead for me? But why? I have done nothing wrong, Your Majesty.

MUMTAZ MAHAL

What could be worse than spreading an inferior religion?

RODREGUIZ

The religion of Christ is the most ennobling...

MUMTAZ MAHAL

(Forcefull) No, never.

RODREGUIZ

It has been proved time and time...

MUMTAZ MAHAL

Then prove it, this time.

RODREGUIZ

I certainly can — through argument.

MUMTAZ MAHAL

That'll take too long. Choose something shorter.

RODREGUIZ

Will a riddle do?

MUMTAZ MAHAL

Yes.

RODREGUIZ

Who'll solve it?

MUMTAZ MAHAL

I will. What are the conditions?

RODREGUIZ

If it be solved correctly by Your Majesty, I'll gladly submit myself to any order that's passed... but if it is solved incorrectly or left unsolved, I propose that I be set free.

MUMTAZ MAHAL

I don't have to accept this, but I am. Let me hear it.

RODREGUIZ

One more condition: it must be solved before I finish saying the rosary.

(He raises his rosary.)

SHAH JAHAN

Rosary? It looks like the necklace I once gave you.

RODREGUIZ

(Coolly) I don't deny it.

SHAH JAHAN

(Hotly) Oh, you don't, you scoundrel!

MUMTAZ MAHAL

Silence! *(To Rodreguiz)* Give me the riddle.

RODREGUIZ

A traveller in a foreign country met two strangers, one of whom was asleep and the other awake. I ask: from which of the two, ought the traveller to seek his way?

ASAF KHAN

(Puzzled) Is this a religious riddle?

RODREGUIZ

(While saying his rosary) Very much so.

MUMTAZ MAHAL

(To Rodreguiz) Hold up the rosary so that we know the count.

(Long pause while RODREGUIZ counts the beads.)

Christ is alive and awake/ The devout Muslims say/ While Mohammed is asleep/ Till the Judgement Day. Something in it... yes, there is... something about being asked the way from a... surely, the traveller can't ask a sleeping man. *(Snaps her fingers)* Yes, padre, I've got it. Listen. The traveller had to wait for the sleeping man to awake, because the man already awake... that's Christ... was himself waiting for the man asleep... that's Mohammed... to wake up so that he could ask him the right way.

RODREGUIZ

(Nervous) I didn't understand.

MUMTAZ MAHAL

(Quietly) The man sleeping was Mohammed, and the man awake was Christ. Not only the traveller but also Christ had to wait for Mohammed to wake up. That means Mohammed is superior to Christ.

RODREGUIZ

(Collapsing) Oh God, the riddle is solved, but against the Christians. Even the Father Superior didn't know, or he lied, when he said it could only be solved in our favour. Oh, Jesus Christ, son of God —

MUMTAZ MAHAL

(Angered) Even now you persist in believing in the inferior prophet. Let's see how he saves you as Shah Jahan strikes you with his sword.

SHAH JAHAN

(Aghast) Strike him? No. You can't mean it.

MUMTAZ MAHAL

I do.

SHAH JAHAN

Strike a religious man in cold blood? Please... let's not take this game too far.

ASAF KHAN

(Puzzled) What kind of a game?

MUMTAZ MAHAL

(To Asaf Khan*)* Don't listen to him.

SHAH JAHAN

(To Mumtaz Mahal,*appealing)* Listen to reason, please, this just can't be done.

MUMTAZ MAHAL

Whatever I say shall be done. I sit on the throne.

SHAH JAHAN

There has to be *(improvising)*... has to be a decree.

MUMTAZ MAHAL

I'll write it. Now.

SHAH JAHAN

A royal decree.

ASAF KHAN

Signed and sealed... the royal seal.

MUMTAZ MAHAL

Who has the seal?
(She looks at Asaf Khan.*)*

ASAF KHAN

I don't have it.
(SHAH JAHAN begins fidgeting with one of his rings and is about to slip something into a side-pocket of his robe.)

MUMTAZ MAHAL

(To Shah Jahan*)* What's that?

SHAH JAHAN

Nothing... nothing... just a ring.

MUMTAZ MAHAL

(Sarcastic) Which happens to bear the royal seal. *(Commanding)* Let me see it... Hurry!
(SHAH JAHAN moves forward reluctantly.)
Faster. Walk faster!
(SHAH JAHAN climbs the steps and holds the ring before her.)
Give it to me!

SHAH JAHAN

Take it.
(SHAH JAHAN extends his hand. As MUMTAZ MAHAL swings out her arm, SHAH JAHAN withdraws his hand.)

MUMTAZ MAHAL

(Angered) Ah!

SHAH JAHAN

All right. Try again. If you really want it... grab it.
(MUMTAZ MAHAL, furious, swings out one arm while levering herself up to snatch the ring. As SHAH JAHAN again withdraws his hand, MUMTAZ MAHAL loses balance.)

ASAF KHAN

Careful! Hold!
(He rushes forward.)

SHAH JAHAN

(Stepping forward to hold her) Oh Allah!
(MUMTAZ MAHAL falls off the steps with a wild cry as the stage darkens.)

Scene 3

Few hours later; evening. The Royal Tower, Agra. The model throne lies toppled. MUMTAZ MAHAL, *lying in bed, is surrounded by a* MAID *with a fly swish, a* PHYSICIAN *and* ASAF KHAN. *A* EUNUCH *stands at the entrance. A child wails, off-stage.*

ASAF KHAN

(Muttering) It's never quiet. *(Going to the* Eunuch*)* Ask them to stop that child's wailing.

EUNUCH

(Bowing) Yes, Excellency.
(He leaves.)

ASAF KHAN

(To the Physician, *who is feeling the pulse of* Mumtaz Mahal*)* How is she?

PHYSICIAN

Weak.
(Enter SHAH JAHAN. *All present bow.)*

SHAH JAHAN

(To the Maid*)* Don't mind the bowing; keep the fly-swish waving. *(Looking at* Mumtaz Mahal*)* She looks paler.

PHYSICIAN

She has lost a lot of blood, Your Majesty.

SHAH JAHAN

Quiet. She's moving. *(Kneeling before* Mumtaz Mahal*)* Yes, my Mumtaz. *(To the* Maid*)* Stop. She wants to say something. *(Pause)* She's sleeping again. *(To the* PHYSICIAN *who is mixing powders)* Let me — *(Extends his hand, grasps the goblet)* Here, my Mumtaz — your potion.

MUMTAZ MAHAL

(Weakly) What?

SHAH JAHAN

The potion.

MUMTAZ MAHAL

It's no use, my lord.

SHAH JAHAN

Please —

MUMTAZ MAHAL

No hope... none. Hope is for the new born... my baby. *(To the* Physician*)* How is she?

PHYSICIAN

All right. She'll survive.

SHAH JAHAN

(To the Physician*)* So must my Mumtaz, the forebringer of my children.

PHYSICIAN

I'm trying, Your Majesty.

MUMTAZ MAHAL

It's no use... it's my punishment... for overstepping my bounds.

SHAH JAHAN

No one really overstepped: it was all a game.

MUMTAZ MAHAL

In the beginning, perhaps. But it changed when you held out your hand to lead me to the throne. A sudden fear gripped me then, a fear that my smouldering desire would erupt and overwhelm my discretion. And it did. I'm sorry for that. *(Clutching* Shah Jahan's *hand)* Will you forgive me, my lord?

SHAH JAHAN

There's nothing to forgive, my Mumtaz. Quite the contrary. The fault is all mine: my silly antics caused this. It was I who threw the bait of the royal seal at you who concocted the need for a royal decree.

MUMTAZ MAHAL

That was much later. How did the whole thing begin? Who got you incensed about a game of chess, made you put up stakes, then made you raise them higher and higher?

ASAF KHAN

Why, my child, what made you do it?

MUMTAZ MAHAL

A long festering desire which became urgent when I heard my baby cry in my womb.

SHAH JAHAN

(Puzzled) A baby's cry?

MUMTAZ MAHAL

Don't you know that when a baby cries in the womb, the mother can't survive its birth? It's a cry of death.

SHAH JAHAN

No, it is not. *(Agitated, gets up)* Ask them. *(To the* Maid*)* Ask her. *(No response)* Or him. *(Turns to the* Physician*)* Is it? *(The* PHYSICIAN *looks at him sheepishly, then lowers his head.)* So what, even if it be true? The fact is that the baby did not cry in her womb. She imagined it. *(To* Mumtaz Mahal*)* It must have been a dream, Mumtaz. May be, you heard the baby cry in the womb, but was it in a dream. Please don't make it up to relieve me of my guilt for having caused that accident. Please.

MUMTAZ MAHAL

I never can remember my dreams, so it must have been real, for I remember it well. And my imagination is much too poor and earthy.

SHAH JAHAN

So stay on earth with me, and make my life rich.

MUMTAZ MAHAL

I've given all I can, my lord. *(Brooding)* For a while I was like the rocket aglow, lighting up the whole sky. *(Eloquent)* I sat on the throne and ruled.

SHAH JAHAN

(Kissing her hands) You fascinate me. Please live with me longer; give me a chance to discover you more.

MUMTAZ MAHAL

My children have something of me. *(Moaning)* I want to see them, to say good-bye.

SHAH JAHAN

Don't say that, please.

MUMTAZ MAHAL

I want my children.

SHAH JAHAN

All right. *(To the* Maid*)* Bring the children, all of them.

MAID

(Bowing) This moment, Your Majesty.
(She leaves.)

MUMTAZ MAHAL

(Gripping Shah Jahan's *arm)* Promise me something.

SHAH JAHAN

Anything you say.

MUMTAZ MAHAL

Please don't marry again.

SHAH JAHAN

I won't, I promise.

MUMTAZ MAHAL

And please grow some hard realism. Don't be afraid to fight mud with mud.

SHAH JAHAN

Yes. *(Kisses her)* Now rest.

MUMTAZ MAHAL

Re...st...
(She dies.)

SHAH JAHAN

(Calling) Physician!
(The PHYSICIAN *feels her pulse, then quietly drops her arm and begins to cover her face with a sheet.* SHAH JAHAN *uncovers her face.)*
She needs fresh air. Let her breathe freely.

PHYSICIAN

(Sadly) She's past breathing.

SHAH JAHAN

No!

PHYSICIAN

The Empress is dead, Your Majesty.

SHAH JAHAN

No!
(Looks at Mumtaz Mahal; *then to the* Physician*)* She's fast asleep... her deep sleep... after a painful child birth.
(He gets up and drifts to front-stage like a lost man, muttering. General wailing breaks out, as lights dim. Back-

stage darkens. The MAIDS *enter, and start wrapping* Mumtaz Mahal's *corpse.)*
Silence! *(Wailing ceases.)*
Let my Mumtaz sleep! Ssh... I shouldn't shout: it'll disturb her.
(Silent speech as front-stage darkens.)

Scene 4

A few hours later. Open Space. A cloudy night. Occasional moonlight reveals a river in the background. Intermittent night sounds – jackals howling, frogs croaking, insects chirping – fill the air. SHAH JAHAN *enters carrying* Mumtaz Mahal *wrapped in white sheets, followed by* ASAF KHAN, *dressed in white.*

ASAF KHAN
Please Shah Jahan, please...
*(*SHAH JAHAN *stops, looks back.)*
Let's return to the Fort, please.
SHAH JAHAN
Huh?
ASAF KHAN
There'll be chaos when they discover her body missing from the Royal Tower. Please. Give her to me: I'll carry her back. *(No response)* Or, at least, let me help. You must be tired.
SHAH JAHAN
(Putting her down tenderly) Yes, I'm tired of it all.
(Sits down) Let me have the box.
ASAF KHAN
You've had enough for an evening. Please, don't overdo it. It's your first time.
SHAH JAHAN
First or last, present or past, what difference does it make?
(Getting up) Give it to me.

ASAF KHAN

If you insist. But, please, think of me. Should something happen to you here, how could I manage to carry you both? I'm old, very old.

SHAH JAHAN

Old or young, meek or bold; black or white, day or night; what difference does it make? Give it to me.

ASAF KHAN

(Unfolding his cloth-belt) All right. *(Stops unfolding)* Look at the sky, the clouds heavy with rain.

SHAH JAHAN

(Shouting) Then let it rain! Let it wash away my misery! For you're keeping my opium away. It dissolves my grief, fires my imagination, spins my mind round and round. *(Sways his head)* Then numb. *(Pause)* Give it to me!

ASAF KHAN

(Nervously handing over the box) Yes, Your Majesty.
(SHAH JAHAN grabs the box, opens it.)

SHAH JAHAN

Nothing. *(Searches frantically)* Not a pill, not even a grain. *(Throwing the box)* Give it.

ASAF KHAN

There's no more, Your Majesty. Not here — with me.

SHAH JAHAN

Then go and get it.

ASAF KHAN

To leave Your Majesty in this wilderness...

SHAH JAHAN

Wilderness? *(He howls like a jackal)* Go and get it!

ASAF KHAN

(Really shaken) Yes.
(He leaves briskly.)

SHAH JAHAN

Wilderness! *(Howls like a jackal, then sniffs the ground – and the corpse)* The perfume... of roses. Her favourite perfume. *(Sniffs more)* It's without fragrance... stale... dead. Perfume dead. Dead? *(Surprised)* Listen. *(Echo of his words)* That's my voice. I said: Mumtaz dead. *(Pause)* I thought I could never say the words. But I did.

(Looking at Mumtaz Mahal*)* So, you are dead, and I am alive. Yet we share something. Both of us became the victims of irony. You manoeuvred me into a tight noose so well that I was forced to grasp your lesson about outfoxing the foxes. But who did I practise your lesson on... first? YOU. Of all people, you — the one I loved most. And you, who believed in the strength of man's will, submitted to superstition. Irony won, and we lost. Irony and death. *(Night sounds.)*

(Hysterical) Death, be cursed! *(Pause)* Cursed? But no, you hold my precious wife. I shouldn't curse you then. I should try to make my peace with you, offer you a gift or two: perhaps end up glorifying you. Not you — really. For, thus I'd be glorifying my Mumtaz. *(To* Mumtaz Mahal, *as if promising)* I'll live to glorify you, but it'll be a hard life: lonely, listless, without zest or vigour, for my vigour died with you. Now there's nothing in me but a vacuum.

(Sits down; stares at Mumtaz Mahal*)* How beautiful — her face glistening in the moonlight! That brow, those sensuous lips. I'll never tire of looking at her face. *(Night sounds)* But no, I should bury her, protect her from the animals. *(Claws the earth, throws it over her sheets)* Oh, I'm spoiling her sheets. Where's the hearse? *(Calls)* Asaf Khan! Asaf Khan! *(No response)* Oh, my head spins. *(Sits)* I may as well lie down... until he comes. *(Lies down.)*

How wonderful the sky looks! The clouds pushed now here, now there, merging, emerging, breaking off. Look at that elephant... with a fox lying low... Lie low, she said wisely, when I wanted to attack Shahriyar. The fox clawing away from below... the elephant is torn apart... black birds on a tree and beyond the tree a building... with a dome. What a dome! *(Gets up. Shakes* Mumtaz Mahal*)* Look, a perfect dome with minarets around it. *(Brief pause)* But you don't look! You don't say anything. *(Lies down)* The building is growing, emerging from behind a line of dark trees. Is that your home now? Is that where you are waiting for me? Up there? *(Getting up.)*

Then I'll bring the building down; I'll anchor it to the earth. *(Rises)* Where? *(A rumble in the sky)* Not here. No. *(Looks around)* There, where the river bends. Your home will have a river at the back and a pool in the front. Your home, your monument! *(Calls)* Asaf Khan! Call the architects, the builders. *(Blows the whistle)* I have the design of a monument so beautiful it'll lure the onlooker, it'll make him think of death as restful, desirable. And I'll make it of white marble, cold and hard as death. It'll be perfect — like my Mumtaz. *(Another rumble in the sky)* Get the architects, Asaf Khan!

VOICE

(Off-stage) Like a mass of Himalayan glacier, shaped by natural forces, with glinting minarets, in the moonlight, with a blue curtain in the back, tall cedars framing it in their stalks... glittering... glorious... glorious.

SHAH JAHAN

(Excited) Glorious... glorious... I have it... It's come... the cloud... the cloud is anchored.

(Severe thunderstorm. Lightning reveals an outline of a maginficent monument on the horizon.)

(Ecstatically) The House of Mumtaz! Taz. Taj. Taj Mahal.

CURTAIN

APPLY, APPLY, NO REPLY

A Play in One Act

CHARACTERS

(In Order of Appearance)

GOUR
SUBODH NAYAK
TARUN BOSE
ANIL ROY

APPLY, APPLY, NO REPLY

First presented at the Maximus Club, London, on 14 June 1976, with the following cast:

SUBODH NAYAK	Renu Setna
TARUN BOSE	Roshan Seth
ANIL ROY	Madhav Sharma
GOUR	Billy Uddin

SEVERAL YOUNG AND MIDDLE-AGED MEN

Directed by Doyne Byrd

First transmitted on BBC-2 by the British Broadcasting Corporation, London, on 12 June 1976, with the following cast:

SUBODH NAYAK	Dev Sagoo
TARUN BOSE	Robert Ashby
ANIL ROY	Roshan Seth
GOUR	Billy Uddin

SEVERAL YOUNG AND MIDDLE-AGED MEN

Directed by Mark Cullingham

Produced by Anne Head

APPLY, APPLY, NO REPLY

A hot and humid summer afternoon in Calcutta. A second-rate café in the north-central area of the city. A few wooden tables, with rickety legs, surrounded by small, armless chairs. A table fan in a corner whirrs noisily to counter heat as well as flies. A few people, all male – some young and others middle-aged – variously dressed, are sitting, listlessly, drinking tea or soft drinks, and/or conversing.

Somewhere, a transistor radio is broadcasting Hindi film songs; but the music is drowned by the hum of the fan. The place is unkempt: the cement floor is strewn with cigarette butts, used match-sticks and food particles.

The walls carry a few calendars. One of these – marked 'Subhash Fabrics' – shows a young man in a smart Western suit about to hug a young woman in a blouse and a long skirt. Another shows a couple, dressed smartly, but informally, in Indian clothes, playing chess with the man smoking Wills Navy Cut Cigarettes.

It is siesta time and the atmosphere is languid. Only GOUR —a slim sixteen year old boy-waiter in short pants and a dirty shirt —with an ever-present, somewhat foolish smile and a brisk walk, provides a contrast.

SUBODH NAYAK, *a small, slim, intelligent-looking man of twentythree, in an unpressed long white shirt and loose pyjamas, is sitting at one of the tables, and reading a single sheet of* The Statesman, *a local English language newspaper. His notebook and loose papers are spread out on the table.*

Presently SUBODH *feels hot. He wipes his perspiration with a handkerchief, and looks in the direction of the table fan. It is on, but is not going round on its axis, as it should.*

SUBODH *looks in the direction of* GOUR *– the boy-waiter who moves like a panther – to catch his eye but fails.*

SUBODH

Aijay!

(GOUR looks at SUBODH, who points in the direction of the fan.

GOUR *smiles his familiar smile, and proceeds to the fan. Soon, all eyes are focused on* Gour. *Without switching off the fan, he turns the knob at the back of the motor. The fan resumes its sideways motions. The* CUSTOMERS *return to their drinks and aimless gossip.* GOUR *smiles triumphantly in the direction of* SUBODH, *who smiles back.* SUBODH *then returns to his news-sheet.*

Intermittent thunder rends the air.

GOUR *arrives with a glass of water, and places it on* Subodh's *table with a flourish.* SUBODH *puts the paper down with a gesture, which says that he has finished reading it.* GOUR *registers the fact and leaves. He looks around and finds a sheet of the newspaper lying in a corner. He brings it to* SUBODH *who gives the sheet a glance).*

SUBODH

Na! Situation vacant. *Chakree Khalee. Chakree.*

(GOUR smiles his special smile, and looks in the direction of another table. They see a young man in profile, bent over a sheet of the newspaper, scribbling something on a piece of paper. They exchange a glance of understanding; and SUBODH *put his hands on the newly arrived sheet as* GOUR *collects the one* SUBODH *has just finished reading.)*

GOUR

Kee?

SUBODH

Cha.

GOUR

(Practising his limited English vocabulary) Okay.

(SUBODH begins to read his sheet without much enthusiasm. He stops, looks around aimlessly then focuses on the calendar marked 'Subhash Fabrics'. He

*starts day-dreaming, visualizing himself as the young man
in the glossy calendar in circumstances that will remain,
forever, beyond his reach.
The fan ceases to oscillate; temperature rises.* SUBODH
*perspires; his spell is broken. He wipes off his perspiration,
and casts a few hard looks around. He finds the other
young man gone, and the 'desired' newspaper sheet lying
on the table. He fetches the sheet and begins to study it.*
GOUR *brings a cup of tea.*
SUBODH, *immersed in his newspaper sheet, sips absent-
mindedly. He burns his tongue, and puts the cup down
abruptly.)*

SUBODH

Shala!
*(*GOUR *giggles, covers his mouth with his hand and walks
away.* SUBODH *resumes his perusal of the sheet, and
finds an appropriate job to apply for. He folds a generous
margin on the left side of his blank foolscap paper, and
prepares to write with some ceremony.*

SUBODH *begins. But the indigenously made ball-point pen
either fails to write or leaks profusely. After having
managed to write a few lines, he stops. Cautiously, he
pours tea into the saucer, peasant-like, and sips from it.
Despite the fan, he perspires. His perspiration makes a
mark on his writing paper. He dries his hand by rubbing it
against his loose pyjamas, and resumes. A few more lines,
and a sip of tea – this time direct from the cup. He resumes
writing. A pair of dark spectacles' clip-ons, held by a hand,
appears on his table. The wrist is adorned with an
expensive watch.* SUBODH *looks up, physically and
metaphorically, to* Tarun Bose, *his friend.* TARUN *has a
largish, round face, with a thin well-trimmed moustache
and glasses. He is above average in height and girth and is
the same age as* Subodh. *He is smartly dressed in
fashionable trousers and bush-shirt, and well-polished,
trendy shoes.)*

TARUN

Monsoon today: the first rain. *(He sits down and wipes his face with an expensive handkerchief)* Today, definite.

SUBODH

So you said yesterday.

TARUN

(A bit pompously) I always say the same thing.

SUBODH

Like I'm always writing the same application.

TARUN

But for a different job.

SUBODH

Which never comes.

TARUN

(Reassuring) It will; it will. Remember the King Bruce of Scotland? And the spider?

SUBODH

'Try and try again'. He tried only seven times. But — myself?

(He gives a deep sigh of despair and self-pity, and sips tea. TARUN looks at Subodh's writing paper.)

TARUN

At least today you've found something to apply for.

SUBODH

(With a faint, bitter smile) My luck. *(Picking up the application with bitter eloquence)* Sir! Dear Sir, Respected Sir, Most honourable Sir, Revered Sir... With reference to your advertisement regarding *(mumbles a few words)* in *The Statesman* dated *(mumbles a few word)* I beg to offer my services *(mumbles a few words)...*

(He hands his application to TARUN as if he were his future employer. TARUN takes the application.)

TARUN

(Reading) Most Revered Sir. *(Pause)* That's a bit...

SUBODH

(Sarcastic) Mild.

TARUN

Where's the advertisement?

(SUBODH gives him the newspaper sheet, and shows him the advertisement. A threatening rumble in the sky.)
(Reading) 'A reputable Calcutta-based pharmaceutical firm requires the services of a Purchace Assistant *(mumbles a few words)...*Storekeeper *(mumbles a few words)* Table Machine Operator *(mumbles a few words)...*'

SUBODH

No, no; low down.

TARUN

(Reading slowly) Typing-cum-Filing Clerk: minimum, graduate, preferably with experience.
(He stops reading, and looks at Subodh, and then at his application.)
(Subconsciously patronising) Typing Clerk. Why are you writing this?

SUBODH

Keep reading.

TARUN

(Reading) 'Apply in your own handwriting mentioning the position being sought in block letters, and a photograph, non-returnable *(mumbles a few words)...* within seven days.'
(GOUR arrives, wipes the table with a dirty, smelly piece of cloth, picks up the empty cup and looks at Tarun.)
Aekta coke.

GOUR

(In a mock Ameican accent) Coke!

TARUN

Khub thanda.

GOUR

(With a wide smile) Okee-dokee.
(He then looks at Subodh.)

TARUN

Doota coke.

SUBODH

No, not for me.

TARUN

Sweets, then?

(SUBODH shrugs his shoulders.)

Aekta coke, khub thanda; aek plate burfee.

(GOUR leaves. TARUN takes out a packet of cigarettes from the breast pocket of his bush-shirt. He offers a cigarette to SUBODH, who hesitates. TARUN insists, SUBODH agrees. TARUN strikes a match, Indian style i.e. away from him but it does not light. Matches are of poor quality, and the air from the fan makes matters worse. A few trials, and then success. The two friends take a few quick puffs.)

SUBODH

Your moustache is looking funny.

(TARUN feels it with his hand.)

TARUN

I know, but there was no time. *(Pause)* I shouldn't have started fiddling with it in the morning.

SUBODH

You should leave such things for a Sunday.

TAURN

I often do. *(Smoking)* Such a botheration to be working on a Saturday.

SUBODH

Not working at all is a bigger botheration.

TARUN

But you have the coaching.

SUBODH

(Slowly, bitingly) One private tuition for one hour per day.

TARUN

But it'd help to be a teacher. That way you get more tuitions.

SUBODH

As bribes from parents.

TARUN

That's how the system works.

(He picks up Subodh's application.)

(Reads) I beg to place here-in-with below my bio-data for your kind and sympathetic consideration.

(He puts the application down on the table, and looks at it.)
Make it simple, *bhaee.*

SUBODH
(Part envious, part sarcastic) You do it — with your St.
Xavier's English.
*(*TARUN *picks up* Subodh's *ball-point pen.)*
Better use your pen. Mine is made in India.
*(*TARUN *takes out his flashy looking ball-pen, – marked
'Made in Hong Kong' – and begins to scribble.)*

TARUN
Herewith please find my particulars.
*(*SUBODH *overcomes his lack of interest in the exercise
and considers the sentence for a while.)*

SUBODH
Or, I submit my particulars ...No — my particulars are as
follows.
(Writes this down and studies.)

TARUN
Aha! *(Approvingly)* That's good. Simple. *(Reads)* My
particulars are as follows:
Name: Subodh Nayak; Father's name and occupation:
Vaidyanath Nayak.
(Pause.)

SUBODH
Proceed.

TARUN
Father's occupation?

SUBODH
Write it, if I forgot.
*(*TARUN *writes.)*

TARUN
(Reads, sensitively) Vaidayanath Nayak, peasant.

SUBODH
(Sharply) No. Farmer.
*(*TARUN *makes the correction. Intermittent thunderstorm.
GOUR arrives with coke and a plate of sweets. TARUN sips
coke, and SUBODH bites into a sweet.)*

GOUR

(To Subodh, *smiling)* Okee-dokee?

SUBODH

Okay.

(GOUR, smiling effusively, leaves.)
The bloody thing is stale.

TARUN

What else to expect in a place like this?

SUBODH

It is certainly not the Grand Hotel.
(An embarrassed TARUN retreats to the application.)

TARUN

(Reading) Age: 22 years and 10 months. *(Pause)* And three days — to be exact.

SUBODH

Five days. *(Seriously)* Five, by the time I finish rewriting and take it on foot, to *The Statesman* office, and the advertiser receives it — along with hundreds of other applications.

TARUN

Who else can produce academic qualifications like: *(Reading)* Passed Secondary Education Final Examination in 1970 in the First Division and secured a special Government scholarship; passed Bachelor of Arts Examination of Calcutta University, with Honours in History, in 1974, in the Higher Second Class. Technical qualification: I know touch-typing. Speed 45 wpm. *(Slowly)* Wpm?

SUBODH

Words per minite.

TARUN

Better say — words per minute.
(SUBODH shrugs his shoulders. TARUN writes.)
(Reading) Testimonials: Original copies will be produced during the interview if granted.

SUBODH

(Bitterly) IF, I capital, F capital.

TARUN

You have said nothing about your job experience.

SUBODH

What job?

TARUN

Private tuitions.

SUBODH

That's no job, ninety rupees per month. Enough to pay for tea and cigarettes, and a share of a dark and dingy room in a dark and dingy slum: just enough to keep an honest, able-bodied man of education, out of mischief — *(with a wry smile)* out of harm's way — as Nakul Chatterjee, my teacher of English in the secondary school, would have put it.

TARUN

You're in a bad mood today.

SUBODH

Yes, my student — my one and only student — is pushing off with his family to the cool heights of Darjeeling next week. That'll be the end of my job experience.

TARUN

Something else will come up.

SUBODH

From where?
(TARUN is speechless. He sips coke. Intermittent rumble in the sky.)

TARUN

(Catching at a silver lining) At last you'll be free to go to your village to see your parents.

SUBODH

(Bitterly) What freedom!

TARUN

Any news about your father?

SUBODH

No. I'm worried.
(Intermittent thunderstorm.)

TARUN

It is a big problem, this job business — you'd agree.

SUBODH

Who am I to agree or disagree?

TARUN

There's a surfeit of qualified people, and competition is tough.

SUBODH

There is no competition; that is the problem. *(With some heat)* Most of these advertisements are bogus, a ritual. The jobs are alredy fixed.

TARUN

That's what I say. It helps to know the right people, the Bengal Club, or the Tollygunge.

SUBODH

(With some irritation) But these bloody advertisements are always under a box number.
(He picks up the sheet.)
(Reading) Apply Box 2340, *The Statesman,* Calcutta, 700001...Box 2338, *The Statesman*...Box 24 —
(TARUN is struck with an idea and snaps his fingers.)

TARUN

Wait. *(Excited)* You know Pradeep? Pradeep Ghosh?
(SUBODH looks unsure.)
That tall lean fellow, with glasses — like this...
(He moves his spectacles to the tip of his nose.)
The one who went around the college reciting his poems like *(gesturing)* 'Your red lips, Juliet, are not so red/
As stained Calcutta streets...'
(SUBODH is still unable to place him.)
The one who lives in Tollygunge, near the film studios. A damn good batsman, runs like a deer.

SUBODH

Yes, yes. I remember, we played against their team once.

TARUN

And he kept hitting boundaries.

SUBODH

What about him?

TARUN

I met him in Park Street the other day. He has got a job in *(with a flourish)* the advertising department of *The Statesman.*

(SUBODH feels envious and shows it.)
SUBODH
But he failed his B.A examination.
TARUN
Never mind. Now, there's somebody who can help. He can tell us the name of this — *(picking up the newspaper sheet, and reading)* 'Reputable Calcutta-based pharmaceutical firm'.

SUBODH
And then?

TARUN
(Smugly) Leave the rest to my father, and his friends at the Bengal Club.
(For the first time, SUBODH *looks cheerful – and excited.)*
SUBODH
That sounds like a good plan, a very good plan *(with a revived scepticism)* if it is successful.

TARUN
It will be, it will be. *(He stubs his cigarette)* Do you know what my mother said the other day?
SUBODH
No, I'm not all-knowing.

TARUN
(Patronising) Omniscient — is the word. *(*SUBODH *nods.)*
She said, 'That Subodh — that shy friend of yours — the one with a thin face. Why don't you invite him round to a meal one day?'

SUBODH
How did she know I was shy?

TARUN
Because you didn't eat all your sweetmeats at the naming ceremony of my nephew.

SUBODH
How did she notice? The drawing room was full up with people.

TARUN
Women have their ways. They notice what they want to — without really looking.

(A thunderstorm, followed by a heavy downpour, the first rain of the monsoon. Many of those inside the café go to the entrance to have a glimpse of the rain. Others stop chattering and listen with smiling, relieved faces, to the sound of the falling rain. They fail to notice that following the thunderstorm the dim electric bulb splattered and went dead and the fan stopped. An excited GOUR runs out to wet himself in the rain.)

GOUR

(Off-stage) Bishti, bishti!
(A self-satisfied TARUN smiles widely.)

TARUN

What did I say? First rain today, definite.

SUBODH

(Brooding) I hope the rain spreads to my village.

TARUN

It's bound to.

SUBODH

My father needs work, field-work.
(An effusive TARUN offers a cigarette to SUBODH, who refuses. He lights his own. He picks up the flashy ball-point pen.)

TARUN

Now —
(He rearranges Subodh's application on the table.)
Job experience?

SUBODH

I have been tutoring a student —

TARUN

Since when?

SUBODH

For the past nine months.

TARUN

Say a year.
(He writes.)
(Reading) For the past one year, I have been tutoring a student —
(He looks at Subodh.)

SUBODH

(Withdrawing into his shell) You know the details. It was you who got me the job.

(TARUN feels a bit peeved, but controls himself. He resumes writing.)

TARUN

(Reading) For the past one year, I have been tutoring a student preparing for the Secondary Final Examination in English, Mathematics and History.

SUBODH

(Somewhat bitterly) At ninety rupees a month.

TARUN

That's not necessary.

(GOUR arrives with a transistor radio which is broadcasting a cricket commentary. He places it on the table.)

GOUR

Cricket. *(Smiling)* England!

TARUN

(Suddenly remembering) The Test Match! *(Looking at his watch)* It must be eleven forty-five in Manchester.

(They both listen to the commentary while GOUR stands uncomprehending. He collects an empty coke bottle and a plate, and leaves. Presently another figure arrives at the table. He is ANIL ROY, a young man in his mid-twenties, of average height and looks, in dirtyish looking shirt and loose pyjamas, which are soaked with rain. He has a carrier bag in his hand.

TARUN and SUBODH are too engrossed in listening to the cricket commentary to notice Anil's arrival. ANIL moves a chair noisily, and sits down. He wants to say something to Subodh, but can't manage it yet.)

ANIL

Cricket is the opium of the Indian petty bourgeoisie.

(SUBODH looks up at him.)

SUBODH

Arré tumi!

(Gets up and hugs Anil*) Kee khabar? Bhalo acheesh?*

ANIL

Han!

(ANIL extends his hand to Tarun.*)*

TARUN

(Shaking Anil's *hand limply)* Politics again.

ANIL

And again.

(SUBODH turns down the radio.)

TARUN

Better dry yourself first. *(He looks in the direction of the fan.)* The bloody thing is off again.

SUBODH

The whole electric supply must be off.

(ANIL dabs his face with a dry handkerchief, then takes out a comb from a side-pocket of his long shirt and combs his hair perfunctorily.)

ANIL

(Mock-seriously, gesturing with a comb in hand) Take heart, fellow-citizens, our bat-wielding warriors are fighting valiantly in the field of Old Trafford in Manchester, across the seven seas, to save the honour of Indian nationalism. *(Seriously)* That's what counts, upholding bourgeois nationalism, not *(pointing to the fan)* keeping this thing running.

TARUN

You're a sarcastic soul.

ANIL

Satirical. I used to read a lot of Swift and Wilde.

TARUN

Before Marx mesmerized you.

ANIL

Me and many others. *(Pause)* And there'll be many, many more.

TARUN

(Patronizingly) But Marx is out of date.

ANIL

How would you know? You've never studied him.

TARUN

I have. *(ANIL cannot hide his surprise)* We discussed him in our Moral Science class at St. Xavier's.

ANIL

So, the holy fathers gave you their Marx in easily digestible capsules.

TARUN

We discussed Marx and Marxism.

ANIL

And the conclusion was?

TARUN

That the urge to own private property is something innate to human nature.

ANIL

(With a condescending smile) That's why one third of the human race today has abolished the institution of private property!

(GOUR arrives, flashes his smile, and puts his hand on the transistor.)

GOUR

Cricket, no?

ANIL

Na! Neeyé jao.

TARUN

(To Anil*)* Tea? Coke?

ANIL

Water, simple and pure. *(To* Gour*) Jal.*

TARUN

(To Gour*)* Coke. *(He looks at* Subodh.*)* Two cokes.
(He offers a cigarette to SUBODH *who accepts it, and then to* ANIL, *who refuses.)*
Come on, *bhaee.*

ANIL

(Firmly) I stopped smoking.
(He pulls out a small box from his side-pocket, opens it, takes out bits of chewing tobacco and lime, mixes them, and then puts the mixture into his mouth, between his

gums and cheeks. SUBODH *looks fascinated, but* TARUN
is disapproving. ANIL *notices* Tarun's *discomfiture and
offers him chewing tobacco.)*
(To Tarun, *teasing in a friendly way)* Try it, *baba.*

TARUN

(With open disgust) No.
*(*ANIL *thrusts his plam, carrying chewing tobacco, into the
face of* Tarun.*)*

ANIL

(With a hard face) It's a substitute for food.
*(*GOUR *arrives with two cokes and a glass of water.* ANIL
picks up his glass.)
This *(holding up his tobacco in one hand)* and this *(raising
water in the other hand)* and you get through the day with
only one meal.

TARUN

(Naively) Can you ?

ANIL

Yes, many people do, in the village *(indicating* Subodh*)* we
come from.

SUBODH

When did you arrive?

ANIL

This morning. There is a meeting which I've come —
(suddenly realises Tarun's *presence)* to ...

TARUN

Political?

ANIL

Cultural, *(smiling at* Tarun*)* to discuss Swift and Wilde. *(To*
Subodh*)* And one more thing.
*(He puts his hand into a side-pocket of his shirt, pulls out a
piece of rolled paper and hands it to* Subodh.*)* From your
mother.
*(*SUBODH *takes the piece, unwraps it, and finds an
amulet.)*

SUBODH

(Surprised and puzzled) This belongs to my father — it's
supposed to bring him good luck. *(Pause)* How is he?

ANIL

(Quietly, firmly) Beyond all suffering.

SUBODH

(Ashen-faced) Kee?
(He gets up abruptly.)
(Shouting) Na! Baba! Na! Baba!
(In a fit of hysteria he grabs Anil *by his shoulders and shakes him.)*
(Shouting) Na na na! (Whimpers) Na.
(He lets Anil *go, and slumps into his chair. He sinks his head into his hand, and begins to sob. He beats his head on the table as he cries. All eyes focus on him.*
GOUR *comes to the table, and whispers something to* ANIL *who puts his finger on his lips, and advises quiet. A long momemt of silence, broken by intermittent rumble in the sky. Then somebody in the café raises the volume of the radio; and a BBC cricket commentary fills the air. SUBODH raises his head, and sniffles. TARUN produces his handkerchief. SUBODH takes it and wipes his face. He gets up suddenly.)*

TARUN

(Alarmed) Where are you going?

SUBODH

To make water.
*(*TARUN *feels relieved, and so does* ANIL. SUBODH *leaves.)*

TARUN

Why did you have to tell him here?

ANIL

I went to his room in the bustee. There was nobody there. The neighbours said, try the café: he goes there to read the English paper.

TARUN

(With some understanding) He has been reading for a long time.

ANIL

It's very familiar: I went through it all myself. *(With a forced smile)* Apply, apply; no reply.

(TARUN feels embarrassed, and looks away. GOUR arrives with a cup of tea for Subodh. He covers the cup with the saucer and leaves. The fan comes to life suddenly.)

TARUN

At last!

(He mops up the remainder of the perspiration with his handkerchief. SUBODH arrives. He sits down quietly, and pours tea into the saucer, and sips – something that irritates Tarun.)

SUBODH

(Quietly) Why didn't they inform me earlier?

ANIL

There was no money for a telegram.

SUBODH

A letter?

ANIL

Your mother said it'd only distract your mind from your job. Nothing can bring your father back, she said: Subodh will know when he comes home.

SUBODH

(Softly) When did this happen?

ANIL

About *(thinks)* two weeks... fifteen days back. It was at dusk, when the cattle returns from the fields, with their bells jingling.

SUBODH

There hasn't been much grass in the fields this year, he wrote in his last letter.

ANIL

That's the one I wrote for him.

SUBODH

(Reminiscing) He was such a hard-working soul.

ANIL

Never idle. He kept on weaving baskets as long as he could; and your mother went out to sell them.

SUBODH

Nobody can support a family of four by selling a few baskets each day. You've got to have farm work.

ANIL

I know.

SUBODH

(Defensive, penitent) I've been doing *my* best.

ANIL

He knew that. *(Pause)* You've *always* done your best.

SUBODH

Where has that got me?

ANIL

It has got you a B. A.

SUBODH

(Self deprecating) Second class.

ANIL

Your father could never stop talking about you. In his last days, while his body grew weaker, his imagination became stronger. My son has obtained a teacher's job in Calcutta, he'd tell everybody; he's teaching the children of gentlefolk, *bhadra lok,* of Calcutta, he'd tell them.

SUBODH

And what did they say?

ANIL

Nothing, nothing in particular. Once the landlord's son asked him, 'Why doesn't Subodh send you some money then?' — that was when he sold the last of his brass plates to the landlord to buy some rice — and he replied, 'Subodh will bring it with him all together, when he comes home during the monsoon'.

(SUBODH is overcome with grief. Tears fall down his cheeks. He sips tea.)

SUBODH

(Pensive) I remember when... when I went home after passing my B.A. He took me around the village like a prize bull. Look, he told everyone, the first Nayak ever to get a B.A. degree, and that too from the Great University of Calcutta.

TARUN

His moment of pride.

ANIL

(Bitterly) Only a moment.

TARUN

But a B.A. is for ever, as long as you live.

ANIL

What can you do with it? Eat it twice a day, fried in mustard oil?

TARUN

We have got a plan worked out.

(He places Subodh's *application in front of* Anil *with a flourish.* ANIL *gives it a quick glance.)*

ANIL

(Reading aloud the last paragraph) Should I be favoured with the job prayed for, I beg, I shall spare no pains to justify your selection. *(He smiles sardonically and lets the application fall on the table.)* Should I be favoured with the post applied for, your most honourable Sir, I shall leave no stone unturned to discharge my duties to the entire satisfaction of my superiors.

(He smiles at Tarun *in a way that deeply embarrasses him.)*

TARUN

(Defensive) What's wrong with that?

*(*ANIL *continues to smile.)*

ANIL

How many applications did you make?

TARUN

Me?

ANIL

Yes.

(Pause.)

TARUN

None — if you like to know the truth.

ANIL

What were your marks in the B.A. examination?

TARUN

(Reluctantly) Third Division.

ANIL

(Matter-of-factly) And you have a cushy job with an advertising company.

TARUN

What are you getting at?

ANIL

There you are, a third class B.A. with a job that fetches 1,200 rupees — or is it 1,300? — per month. And there is Subodh Nayak, a B.A. honours, a brilliant student, earning 90 rupees per month, tutoring an idiotic son of an idiotic businessman. Subodh Nayak, who has made a hundred applications —

SUBODH

More than that.

ANIL

More than one hundred applications, with what? — two interviews.

SUBODH

Three.

ANIL

Three interviews in all, none of them successful.

TARUN

(Uneasy and irritated) Of course, we agreed before you came that the situation is difficult. But I'm trying to help him.

ANIL

How many Subodhs can you help? Only a few.

TARUN

Every little bit helps.

ANIL

How long have you been at it — helping?

TARUN

How do you mean? I've known Subodh since the college days.

ANIL

I don't mean individual you, and individual him. I mean your kind. For how long has your kind been 'helping' our kind?

TARUN

I don't understand.

ANIL

You never will.

TARUN

Do you?

ANIL

Yes. One thing I do understand. This system, your system, is rotten, absolutely rotten — beyond repair.

TARUN

There's always hope.

ANIL

Hope is here.
(He raises a clenched fist.)

TARUN

You'll end up in jail.

ANIL

(Defiant) How many of us can you jail?

TARUN

Quite a lot. *(Looking at Subodh)* Anyway, he'll never get mixed up in such things. Would you?

SUBODH

How can you be so certain.

TARUN

Because you are my friend. Besides, you might get killed by mixing up in such politicking.
(SUBODH is about to speak, when –)

ANIL

You die a little every time you write an applicaton like this, Mr. Bose.
(He points to the application.)

SUBODH

My father never mixed in politics; and he got killed.

TARUN

He died.

SUBODH

No; he was killed.

TARUN

He died of starvation.

ANIL

This is treason. Death by starvation was abolished the day the British left, and the Indian bourgeoisie took over.

SUBODH

(Bitterly, but calmly) Vaidyanath Nayak, aged fortyseven, a landless labourer of the village Payercheli, district Midnapore, died of malnutrition on the first of June at six — so reads a report, recorded by an official of the Government of West Bengal.

TARUN

(Trying to be reasonable) But that's the past, Subodh. You have a future ahead of you.

(SUBODH bursts into bitter laughter.)

SUBODH

Future?

(ANIL looks at Tarun.)

ANIL

A future for all those thousands upon thousands of unemployed graduates of West Bengal?

TARUN

So you think you're going to improve the situation through the use of violence?

ANIL

(Coldly) Who killed Vaidyanath Nayak? And ten thousand others like him this season? Whose violence?

TARUN

You're a fanatic.

ANIL

(Firmly, coldly) I am an M.A.; and I'm teaching in a primary school in a village at one-sixth the salary you receive. And, thanks to the bureaucratic ways of your system, I haven't been paid for the last three months.

TARUN

(Defensive) But, at least, you have a job.

ANIL

(Looking at Subodh) He has none.

TARUN

He'll never become like you.

SUBODH

What makes you say so?

TARUN

(Charming) You're my friend, a close friend.
(ANIL puts his arm around Subodh's shoulder.)

ANIL

He and I come from the same village: we are of the same
earth.

TARUN

But he wants to make his life in the city.

ANIL

What life?

TARUN

You shouldn't give up.
*(SUBODH looks hesitant; he turns first to Tarun then to
Anil; and back to Tarun.)*
There's this application.
(He indicates the application.)

ANIL

Waste of time!
*(SUBODH picks up the application, looks at it, and puts it
down.)*

TARUN

Who knows — with a bit of wire-pulling —

SUBODH

You have said that before.

TARUN

What will you do in the village, anyway?

SUBODH

What am I doing here?

ANIL

(Oratorical) While the village calls, while the poor suffer
under the yoke of landlords. Waiting. *(Brief pause)* Waiting
for their sons, their educated sons to return, to speak up, to
fight.
(He clenches his fists.)

TARUN

(Exasperated) Oh, please — stop!

ANIL

You stop! Bourgeois bastard! *Shala!*

TARUN

Shut up, you peasant!
(ANIL rises quickly, grabs TARUN by the collar, and is about to hit him when SUBODH intervenes.)

SUBODH

Anil!
(Others in the café converge around their table. TARUN is sitting still, unruffled.)

TARUN

What's the matter? Don't you like to be called a peasant?
(The point gets through: ANIL loosens his grip.)
Chewing tobacco isn't enough to turn you into a peasant guerrilla, Comrade Anil Roy.

ANIL

Shut up! *(Pause)* Push off!
(He stands threatening over Tarun.*)*

TARUN

You push off. *(Slowly, with relish)* The city is the citadel of the bourgeoisie.
(A defiant ANIL sits down and mutters angrily. TARUN stands up.)
(Coldly) I suggest you leave. And *(looking at his watch)* I'm giving you exactly two minutes.
(SUBODH gets up and tries to persuade Anil.)

ANIL

Shala!

SUBODH

Please, Anil.
(SUBODH touches ANIL who brushes him off angrily.)

ANIL

Keep off!

SUBODH

Please, for my sake.
(ANIL is sitting still and muttering angrily.)

TARUN

(Looking at his watch) One minute to go.

SUBODH

(To Anil*)* Please, Anil, do as he says. *Arré bhaee, ja na.* *(Pause)* Otherwise the police will get hold of you. And you know what happens then? *(Pause) Dada. (*ANIL *gets up to leave.)*

ANIL

(To Tarun*)* We'll make shoes out of the skins of your kind.

TARUN

(Smugly) We're already wearing shoes of the skins of your kind.

*(*ANIL *leaves.* SUBODH *sits down. Others disperse and return to thir seats. Intermittent thunderstorm.* SUBODH *begins to tidy up the table. He puts his notebook and a few sheets of paper together, and moves them to his corner – an indication of his withdrawal from* Tarun. *He picks up his leaky ball-point pen, puts its cap on, and places it next to his notebook and paper, as if emphasising his earlier gesture.* TARUN *picks up the application.)*

If you rewrite this now, and give me a photograph, I'll drop it in at *The Statesman* office on my way home.

*(*SUBODH *takes the application and begins to tear it slowly.)*

(Puzzled) Why?

SUBODH

(Whispering) Why? I've had enough. I'm going back, with Anil.

(He rises, picks up the torn application, and tears it further – slowly, provocatively.)

(Firmly) We'll work to make villages the citadel of the poor — and then encircle the city.

(For the first time TARUN *looks frightened.* SUBODH *goes.)*

CURTAIN

GLOSSARY OF BENGALI WORDS

Aekta	One
Aijay	Oh, you
Arré	Oh
Baba	(lit.) Father; (fig.) Older person
Bhadra Lok	Gentlefolk
Bhaee	(lit.) Brother; (fig.)Friend
Bhalo acheesh?	How are you?
Bishti	Rain
Burfee	Sweetmeat
Chakree	Job
Dada	(lit.) Elder brother; (fig.) Respected friend
Doota	Two
Han	Yes
Ja	Go
Jal	Water
Kee	What
Khabar	News
Khalee	Vacant
Khub	Very
Na	No
Neeyé jao	Take it away
Shala	(lit.) Brother of one's wife; (fig.) Bastard
Thanda	Cold
Tumee	You

A CLEAN BREAK

A Play in One Act

A CLEAN BREAK

CHARACTERS

(In Order of Appearance)

ANWAR HASSAN
RACHEL GREENE
CHRISTOPHER BARR-LOVE
POLICEMAN

A CLEAN BREAK

First presented at the Ravi Shankar Hall, London, on 24 November 1977, by Ramesh Patel, with the following cast:

ANWAR HASSAN	Dino Shafeek
RACHEL GREENE	Miranda Messenger
CHRISTOPHER BARR-LOVE	Gregory de Polnay
POLICEMAN	Raju Patel

Directed by Harbhajan Virdi

A CLEAN BREAK

A warm summer night, somewhere in London. Interior of a twentyfour-hour laundrette. Washing machines, driers, and a coin-operated machine dispensing soap powder. The walls are plastered with notices: how to use a washing machine or a drier, what the charges are, and what to do in case of a breakdown. Directly opposite the entrance is a door marked 'Private'. By its side on the wall, hangs a coin telephone box; and above it, an electric clock. It is nearly one o'clock.

On the wooden bench, near the entrance, a transistor radio is broadcasting a late night phone-in programme on a local commercial station. Two washing machines are running.

ANWAR HASSAN, thirtytwo, an attractive man of Indian origin, is standing near the call-box with the receiver in one hand and coins in the other. He is light brown, with large expressive eyes, shining black hair, and a Leninesque beard. He is in the middle of a discussion on the phone-in programme that is being broadcast by the radio lying on the bench.

ANWAR

(Heatedly) Why do you keep dragging in the country of my birth? What has that to do with the argument? Some of the best known British were born abroad, you know. Lord Butler, the Duke of Edinburgh, Lord Thompson. And Arthur Keostler. And what about Karl Marx, and Friedrich —

GUEST ON THE RADIO PROGRAMME

(Sharply) Marx? That bearded Hun should never have been allowed into this country. He abused our hospitality.

(RACHEL GREEN enters. A slim and sexy woman of twentysix, she is wearing tight jeans and a cleverly cut open neck shirt which enhances her bra-less breasts. She has a handbag in one hand and a coin in the other. She is in a hurry.)

ANWAR

Oh, come now. You can't be serious. Marx abusing British hospitality? How? By offering the world a most perceptive theory of history?

GUEST ON THE RADIO PROGRAMME

Don't exaggerate. Marx had a few things to say about the capitalism of his times. I grant you that. But the world has moved on since — and not in the direction he predicted. Workers are not at the throats of their bosses in Western capitalism. They are equal partners. The *laissez faire* capitalism of the past has created the welfare state of today. And it has fostered movements like Black Power and Women's Liberation —

ANWAR

Ah, but you forget. It was Friedrich Engels who said, 'Within the family, man is bourgeoisie and woman represents the proletariat'. He said that a good hundred years ago. And —

HOST OF THE PROGRAMME

Excuse me, Mr. Hassan; but I have to cut you short. We must have a break here.

ANWAR

Blast!

PRE-RECORDED INSERT

This is the LBC Nightline 261...

(ANWAR puts the receiver down. RACHEL approaches him.)

RACHEL

Excuse me. *(Opening her hand)* Could you change this, please?

(ANWAR feels his pockets, and mutters absent-mindedly.)
It's for fags.

(ANWAR brings out the few coins he has, but these are not enough.)

ANWAR

Sorry.

RACHEL

Shit!

ANWAR

You can smoke mine.
(He offers her a cigarette. She accepts eagerly.)

RACHEL

Thank you.
(She lights his cigarette, then her own. She takes a few quick puffs.)

RACHEL

Excuse me, but I must sit down.

ANWAR

Tired?

RACHEL

Very.
(RACHEL sits down on the bench; ANWAR goes to the washing machines. She takes off her rubber-soled sandal, puts her foot up on the bench, and touches the blister on her little toe gingerly. ANWAR approaches the bench, and looks down at her foot.)

ANWAR

(Softly) Looks bad.
(RACHEL looks at him, and bends her ear.)

RACHEL

(Loudly) I can't hear you.
(She indicates the radio which is blurting out a commercial.)

ANWAR

Sorry.
(He switches off the radio.)

ANWAR

It looks bad, I said.

RACHEL

Yeah.
(She caresses the blister.)
You sound like the guy on the radio just now.

ANWAR

(Smiling) Yes, I'm that guy : Anwar Hassan.

RACHEL

Oh! *(Pause)* You're a Communist, then?

                         ANWAR
No, a Marxist.
(RACHEL takes out a safety pin from her hand bag.)
                         RACHEL
What's the difference?
                         ANWAR
As between a practising Christian and a non-practising
one.
*(RACHEL pierces the blister with the pin. She then fishes
for a tissue paper inside her handbag. ANWAR pulls out
one from his hip pocket and offers it to her. She takes it.)*
                         RACHEL
Thanks.
                         ANWAR
You're brave.
                         RACHEL
So my father used to say.
                         ANWAR
Is he dead?
                         RACHEL
No, he's in New Zealand. Which is as good as being dead.
                         ANWAR
Is that why you left?
                         RACHEL
Damn right. As soon as I could get a passport.
*(RACHEL wipes off the blistery liquid with the tissue paper,
then covers her little toe with it.)*
                         ANWAR
How does it feel?
                         RACHEL
Like having a pee after a long wait outside the loo.
*(ANWAR is startled by the blunt language, but recovers
fast, and manages a polite smile.)*
                         ANWAR
You must have walked far.
                         RACHEL
(Sharply) That's perfectly obvious, isn't it?

ANWAR

(Firmly) Are you always so rude?

RACHEL

No, not to strangers, anyway.
(Uneasy pause.)

ANWAR

Lost your keys, have you?

RACHEL

(Tensely) Why do you want to know?

ANWAR

(Friendly) It happened to me once, you know. And I didn't have enough to book into a hotel.

RACHEL

(Matter-of-factly) So you slept rough?

ANWAR

(Quietly) No.

RACHEL

What did you do then?

ANWAR

(Charmingly; devastatingly) Why do you want to know?

RACHEL

(Recovering) You like playing games?

ANWAR

I like playing at being a mirror.

RACHEL

A murky one.

ANWAR

(Sensitive) So — I should get myself bleached.

RACHEL

That's your hang-up.

ANWAR

(Cut down) Oh.
(Pause. RACHEL smokes.)

RACHEL

(Conciliatory) This is an odd time to be doing your laundry.

ANWAR

I'm travelling tomorrow.

RACHEL

Where to?

ANWAR

(Partly joking, partly serious) Where the action is.

RACHEL

You some kind of travelling revolutionary, are you?

ANWAR

I'm in travel business.

RACHEL

You work for a travel agency?

ANWAR

No, I have my own.

RACHEL

(Amused) A Marxist travel agent?

ANWAR

(Pensively) Anything wrong with that?

(RACHEL gives out a nervous laugh.)

RACHEL

You do look upset.

ANWAR

I didn't mean to. *(Smiling)* Is the toe feeling better now?

RACHEL

Yes, thank you.

(She removes the tissue paper.)

ANWAR

Why did you keep on walking?

RACHEL

To work off my frustration.

ANWAR

At?

RACHEL

(Withdrawing) That's none of your business.

(She looks away, puts her foot down, and notices that one of the two machines has stopped.)

Anyway, your wash is done.

(ANWAR goes to the washing machine which has overflowed.)

ANWAR

Hell! It's like Loch Ness here.
(He half-turns to read the breakdown instructions on the wall. She walks to the machine and gives it a cursory glance.)

RACHEL

Hit it, man.
(Without waiting she hits the machine – hard. It goes.)

ANWAR

The magic touch.

RACHEL

Which had all the sheep on our farm in New Zealand bleating.

ANWAR

(Pulling her leg) Asking for more?

RACHEL

(Seriously) You must be joking.

ANWAR

You'd make a good mechanic.

RACHEL

If only my brother could hear you say that. He'd have a fit.

ANWAR

He'd regard it as an intrusion into the Man's World?

RACHEL

Precisely.

ANWAR

(Scoring a point) Like a Marxist setting up a business?

RACHEL

You don't like to lose?

ANWAR

Do you?

RACHEL

No. *(Peace signal)* Birds of same feather, then.

ANWAR

(Scoring again) Under the skin.
(Pause. RACHEL smokes.)

RACHEL

How did you get into the travel business?

ANWAR

Quite by chance. My cousin had it going. He was doing well; but suddenly he had a yearning for the sun — for Karachi. *(Confidentially)* He was in some kind of fiddle, I think, and got wind that things were hotting up. *(Matter-of-factly)* Anyway, he asked me if I'd like to take over. I gave it a thought, and said, 'Why not?'. At least I'd be my own boss.

RACHEL

(Teasing) With your own fiddle?

ANWAR

Oh no. I'm much too straight. That's what teaching law does.

RACHEL

Where did you teach?

ANWAR

Holborn College.

RACHEL

That seems more your line than flogging airline tickets.

ANWAR

Thank you. *(Pause)* And what's your line?

RACHEL

Film.

ANWAR

What kind?

RACHEL

All kinds. Chris has an independent film company of his own.

ANWAR

Who's Chris?

RACHEL

My boyfriend.

ANWAR

(Disappointed) Oh. *(With some difficulty)* Steady?

RACHEL

We're living together.

ANWAR

And quarrelling.

RACHEL

And making it up.

ANWAR

And quarrelling again, like tonight.

RACHEL

You seem to speak from experience.

ANWAR

I was married once... to a Canadian I met here.

RACHEL

In this laundrette?

ANWAR

Oh no. Madame Tussaud's, of all places.

RACHEL

What happened... to your marriage?

ANWAR

We split — about a year ago.

RACHEL

Any children?

ANWAR

None.

RACHEL

Do you have any regrets?

ANWAR

None.

RACHEL

Any second thoughts?

ANWAR

None.

RACHEL

You sound like a robot.

ANWAR

No. *(Pause)* I expect to sound like a rational human being.

RACHEL

But that doesn't put you above pain.

ANWAR

Of course not.

RACHEL

Was it painful?

ANWAR

What?

RACHEL

The break-up.

ANWAR

No, not really. When you've prepared yourself for something in advance, you immunise yourself against pain — or pleasure.

RACHEL

It sounds very cold and calculating.

ANWAR

I'd say clear and concise. Once you've realised that you've reached the end of the journey with someone, you must find the courage to say, 'This is where we part'. A clean break.

RACHEL

What — if the other person is not ready to part?

ANWAR

And wants to continue the ritual of periodic shouting matches, and clawing at each other's innards and spilling blood, and —

RACHEL

(Cutting in) Capping all that with wrestling in bed?

ANWAR

Treating sex as another form of fighting.

RACHEL

That's what my father and mother used to do.

ANWAR

And you wish to carry on the 'family tradition'?

RACHEL

I don't know. *(Reflective)* There are moments when I think 'clear and concise'. And I see the end of the journey.

ANWAR

With whom?

RACHEL

Chris. *(Pause)* Who else?

ANWAR

(Controlled pleasure) Ah.

(He notices that one of the machines has stopped again. He goes to the machine and hits it hard. It goes. RACHEL *stands up.)*

RACHEL

You think you're somebody special, don't you?

ANWAR

Everybody does.

RACHEL

But some more so than others.

ANWAR

So you want to know whether I'm 'some' or 'others'?

RACHEL

Yes.

ANWAR

What are you?

RACHEL

(Firmly) Don't evade the question like some — slimy Asian.

ANWAR

I like your bluntness. We could do business together.

RACHEL

(Crisply) I'm not ready yet for a return trip to New Zealand.

ANWAR

(With a pronounced North Indian accent) I'll give you cut-rate, madam, rock bottom price.

RACHEL

(Softening) I might manage if that commercial comes through.

ANWAR

Ah, there's money in them commercials.

RACHEL

Sure. Only the chances of getting a contract for one are about as high as winning the football pools.

ANWAR

What do you do in between — winning the pools?

RACHEL

Make other kinds of films.

ANWAR

Jointly?

RACHEL

Yes.

ANAWAR

With you sharing credit with Chris?

RACHEL

Hell, no!

ANWAR

Why not?

RACHEL

Why yes?

ANWAR

You said jointly — meaning equally.

RACHEL

Chris was well established long before I could tell the difference between a dissolve and a fade-in.

ANWAR

(Sarcastically) A piece of knowledge for which you are expected to remain obliged for ever.

RACHEL

Why is it upsetting you?

ANWAR

All exploitation upsets me. Here's a clear example of a man exploiting his woman, appropriating the fruit of her labour.

RACHEL

(Slowly) 'Appropriating the fruit of her labour'. That sounds heavy. Germanic.

ANWAR

Well, Engels was German.

RACHEL

Why don't you come clean, and say you dislike Chris.

ANWAR

(Defensive) Now — now; how could I like or dislike somebody I've never met?
(The phone rings.)

RACHEL

You could. But —

ANWAR

Excuse me.
(He goes to the phone and picks up the receiver.)

ANWAR

Sorry, you have got a wrong number.
(A tense RACHEL switches on the radio. She finds a station broadcasting a dance number.)
It isn't the doctor's. It's a laundrette.
(He puts the receiver down. RACHEL raises the volume of the dance number.)
Would you like to dance?

RACHEL

(Impulsively) Yes.
(They dance.)

RACHEL

What'd a copper make of this?

ANWAR

It'd blow his mind. Surrealism, *a la* Thurber.

RACHEL

Who's he?

ANWAR

Thurber is Thurber.

RACHEL

Very enlightening.
(They dance.)

ANWAR

Where did you meet Chris?

RACHEL

At a party.

ANWAR

A movie moghul's?

RACHEL

A weird painter's, in Notting Hill. A guy who made a killing designing psychedelic jackets for LPs. I took his pictures once for a trendy magazine: one of those rags of the Swinging Sixties, with multicolour typesetting and monochrome pictures.

ANWAR

With you as the staff photographer?

RACHEL

You kidding? They couldn't afford a tea-girl, much less a staff photographer. No, I was a freelance then. 'Have Canon, Will shoot': that was my rallying cry.

ANWAR

Pure Freud.

RACHEL

Oh, Chris adores Freud. You know what? I went to that party wearing a long skirt, blouse and a tie. A tie! So he put me down as butch.

ANWAR

What did you put him down as?

RACHEL

A narcissist, accompanied by a girl of his kind.

ANWAR

A mirror image?

RACHEL

Not really. A French girl, Parisian — high cheekbones, haughty looking — called Genevieve.

ANWAR

Good God! You haven't told me your name yet.

RACHEL

You haven't asked, you male chauvinist.

ANWAR

I am asking now.

RACHEL

Rachel M. Greene.

ANWAR

Butch!

RACHEL

(Wittily) Without Cassidy!

ANWAR

(Acidly) Without Chris.

RACHEL

Chris and you would soon come to blows if you ever met.

ANWAR

I don't think he would use violence.

RACHEL

Oh, he does.

ANWAR

Against you — I suppose.

RACHEL

(Sharing a secret) But he gets as good as he gives.

ANWAR

That's the only way.
(They stop dancing. ANWAR gives her a cigarette. She lights up.)
Where do you think he might be now?

RACHEL

Who?

ANWAR

Chris.

RACHEL

In the flat, I guess.

ANWAR

Fast asleep.

RACHEL

I doubt it. He's such a tense guy, all nerves. There was a time he had to have an injection daily in the backbone.

ANWAR

Why?

RACHEL

To relieve tension. That was before we started to live together.

ANWAR

That helped him, I hope.

RACHEL

Yes, but only for a while. He's so tense and insecure. He's always accusing me of having an affair with one guy or the other. The man is thirtyone; but the way he behaves sometimes, you'd think he was seventeen.

ANWAR

That's what got the row started tonight.

RACHEL

Yeah.
(Pause.)

ANWAR

What happens now?

RACHEL

(Nonchalantly) The same as before. I think, I should phone him. *(Pause)* Should I?

ANWAR

(Shaking his head) It's not for me to say.

RACHEL

He'll be worried.

ANWAR

A guy like him will always be worrying, about something.

RACHEL

Still —

ANWAR

Why not just creep back home quietly?

RACHEL

Creeping back may be all right. But, quiet it won't be. I know that. We'll start all over again. And I don't think I can take any more of it. I've had enough. *(Sighs)* It has been a hell of a day.

ANWAR

(Charmingly) Let me hold your hand. May I?

RACHEL

All right.
(ANWAR holds her hand.)

ANWAR

Your palm is wet.

RACHEL

I know.

ANWAR

You're nervous?

RACHEL

Wouldn't you — in my position?

ANWAR

(To please her) I guess I would.
(Moments of friendly relaxation. She disengages her hand, and gets up.)

RACHEL

Let me talk to David. *(Catching the quizzical look on Anwar's face)* He's an actor friend of ours.

ANWAR

(Looking at his watch) At this time of the night?

RACHEL

I don't think he'd mind.
(She goes to the phone, and dials, but there's no reply. She puts the receiver down, waits a while, and dials again. Still no response.)

RACHEL

Shit! *(To Anwar)* There's no reply.

ANWAR

Perhaps he's out of town.

RACHEL

He can't be. I saw him this evening.

ANWAR

Oh.

RACHEL

He's my ex.

ANWAR

(Light-heartedly) The one you abandoned for Chris. The poor man.

RACHEL

(Seriously) David abandoned me, if you want to know the truth. Darling — he said to me once — acting is so emotionally demanding, you need to charge your batteries every so often; and nothing charges my batteries better than changing my partner.

ANWAR

Now, that's an honest man speaking.

RACHEL

And intelligent. Something you can't say of ninetynine per cent of that lot. Actors are like cattle. That's what Chris would say every time he had to work with them.

ANWAR

Did he ever work with David?

RACHEL

Yes, in one of his documentary dramas. But that was long before either of them knew me.

ANWAR

When did you and David split?

RACHEL

Two years next month. But it wasn't a clean break.

ANWAR

That's obvious. You keep seeing him.

RACHEL

(Happily) David is such fun to be with: extrovert, chatty, a born raconteur. An actor's actor.

ANWAR

The best cure for your depression.

RACHEL

Anybody's depression.

ANWAR

Except Chris's, I suppose. How does he take this?

RACHEL

Badly. But he'd never say so openly. So the whole thing builds up. Then suddenly: boom!

ANWAR

Like tonight.

RACHEL

Yes, he got so hysterical I never got the chance to tell him that I am pregnant.

ANWAR

Who by?

RACHEL

Chris. Who else?

ANWAR

(Smiling) How'd I know?

RACHEL

It's no smiling matter.
(She returns to the bench, and sits down.)
I must have a fag.
(They light up.)

ANWAR

Thanks.

RACHEL

(Nervously) It was only this afternoon that the lab gave me the bad news. I was so upset I had to talk to somebody. Chris was away, filming. So I rang David. We had a few drinks, and then a meal at a Greek restaurant by the Post Office Tower. The food was delicious, and the wine, and David's anecdotes. I felt better, much better. I was pissed. But I got back home all right, ready to plonk into bed. And, there was Chris, in the kitchen, fuming with rage! The moment I uttered the word David, he went berserk. He threw a mug of tea at me. Look!
(She shows him tea spots on her shirt and jeans.)

ANWAR

Then?

RACHEL

I ran out. He came after me. I kept running. I heard a car racing from behind me. Head lights! So I turned into a side street, and then another. I saw a front garden with a hedge. I hid behind the hedge and got my breath back. I rifled my handbag for fags. There was only one left. I smoked it slowly, very slowly. I got tired standing, and went back to the pavement. But every time I saw or heard a car, I froze. I was so tense and miserable and afraid and pissed, I could have cried. And no fuckin' fags! I kept walking, and walking, walking...
(She puts her foot up and looks at it absent-mindedly. Moments of total quietude: one of the washing machines containing Anwar's laundry has finished its task, and the other has broken down.)

ANWAR

How far is your flat from here?

RACHEL

Not too far. Why?
(ANWAR shrugs his shoulders.)

ANWAR

Just... Why don't you phone a girl friend?

RACHEL

At this time of night? *(Pause)* I'd better book into a hotel.

ANWAR

Have you got enough money?

RACHEL

I should have — for one night.
(She takes her wallet from the handbag, and counts the money: two pound notes, a 50-pence coin, and a few small coins.)
Shit! David's fault. He's always sponging off me.

ANWAR

I can lend you some.

RACHEL

Now, what's your line?
(Pause, as RACHEL regards Anwar critically.)
(Indecisively) Can I trust you?

ANWAR

(Firmly) I'm trusting you by offering to lend you some money. Better take it before I change my mind.
(He produces some pound notes from his wallet.)

RACHEL

(Hesitatingly) Okay.
(She takes three pound notes from Anwar's hand, one at a time.)
Thanks — awfully. *(Putting the notes in her wallet)* Where do I return the money?

ANWAR

Here.
(He gives her a visiting card.)
How will you get to a hotel?

RACHEL

I'll walk.

ANWAR

And give yourself another blister? *(Pause)* I can take you in my car — once the wash is done.

RACHEL

Thanks.

ANWAR

But you could save all the money, you know. *(Hesitantly)* You can stay the night in my flat, if you like.

RACHEL

(Sharply) My God, here goes another sexist!

ANWAR

I didn't say you could sleep in my bed.

RACHEL

(Turning around) Why? Does your bed carry a sign 'For Indian Princesses Only'?

ANWAR

(Wearily) You're like these machines: temperamental.

RACHEL

(At a breaking point) I'm just too tired to be consistent. Can't you see that?

ANWAR

Yes. *(Catching sight of one of the machines)* Good God, that one is off again.
(He goes to the machine and hits it. Nothing happens. RACHEL does the same, but to no effect. She opens the machine.)

RACHEL

It's only the last spin left.

ANWAR

Give me a hand, will you?
(Each of them picks up a garment at a time, wrings it, and puts it on top of the adjoining machine. Unknown to them, CHRIS enters. He is thirtyone, tall, well-built with narrow eyes in an attractive, but wooden, face. He is wearing jeans, a denim shirt, and loafers.)

CHRIS

Sorry to interrupt this domestic little scene.
(A startled RACHEL is speechless for a while.)

RACHEL

That's all right. *(Pause)* Oh — this is Anwar...

ANWAR

Hassan.

RACHEL

This is Chris Ba —

CHRIS

(Cutting in) Christopher, if you don't mind

RACHEL

Christopher Barr-Love.

(ANWAR extends his wet hand hesitantly.)

ANWAR

Sorry, my hand —

CHRIS

Please... don't bother. Carry on with the good work.
(He lets out a short nervous laugh. RACHEL and ANWAR resume wringing wet clothes. CHRIS watches.)

RACHEL

(To Chris) How did you know I was here?

CHRIS

I didn't. I was just passing by.

RACHEL

Oh.

CHRIS

I waited for you, hoping you'd be back.

RACHEL

After having chased me by car, and losing me?

CHRIS

(With exaggerated surprise) Car? *(Pause)* What car?

RACHEL

Your car — or ours, to be exact.

CHRIS

I did no such thing. *(Emotionally)* Believe me, darling.

RACHEL

(Softening) But you came running after me?

CHRIS

Yes; only for a short stretch. Then I went back home and waited and waited, feeling miserable, and not knowing what to do.

RACHEL

Well, at least you were at home while I was on the streets.

CHRIS

It was worse being inside — not knowing what to do — waiting for the phone to ring, or the door bell.

RACHEL

(Quietly) Neither of which did.

CHRIS

No. So I went out — to David's.

RACHEL

(Abrasively) You what?

(She stops wringing clothes, and glares at Chris. ANWAR, *looking unperturbed, plods through the pile of clothes.)*

CHRIS

I went to David's. And, that bastard wouldn't let me through the front door. He just stood there, naked to the waist, cursing me for disturbing him at an ungodly hour. *(Mimicking)* 'Do you realise I've got an audition at the BBC at 9.30 in the morning', he said.

RACHEL

And of course you didn't believe him.

CHRIS

Umm... One can never tell... with theatrical types like David: one can never tell. Anyway, the phone rang. 'Go home', he said; Rachel isn't here. So I started to argue with him. 'Piss off', he shouted. I could have punched him.

RACHEL

Why didn't you?

CHRIS

He slammed the door in my face.

RACHEL

Served you right. *(Absent-mindedly)* Why did you go there, anyway?

CHRIS

I thought you might be there.

RACHEL

(Acidly) In bed with him.

CHRIS

(Bashfully) Ah, well... no.

(ANWAR finishes wringing clothes and takes them to a drier.)

RACHEL

And how did you get here?

CHRIS

Couldn't sleep. So I thought I'd stroll around a bit.

RACHEL

You could have taken the sleeping pills.

CHRIS

I'm off them.

RACHEL

Since when?

CHRIS

Since my last visit to Dr. Stein. He told me to stop, for the time being. Didn't I tell you?

(ANWAR approaches Rachel and Chris with a 10-pence piece in hand.)

ANWAR

Excuse me. Could you... 5-pences please.

(CHRIS digs into his pockets and RACHEL into her wallet. CHRIS finds a 5-pence coin and gives it to Anwar. RACHEL can find none.)

RACHEL

Sorry.

(ANWAR offers a 10-pence piece to Chris.)

CHRIS

That's all right.

ANWAR

Thanks.

(ANWAR goes to the drier and feeds it a 5-pence coin. RACHEL returns to the bench to put her wallet back into her handbag.)

ANWAR

I think... *(improvising)* I'll get some cigarettes... A machine over there...

RACHEL

(Enthusiastically) Get some for me too, please. *(To* Chris*)* Can you spare me some change, please. *(*CHRIS *gives some coin to* Anwar.*)*
Benson and Hedges... otherwise... Embassy, Silk Cut. *(*ANWAR *takes the money.)*

ANWAR

Okay.
(He leaves.)

CHRIS

How long has this been going on?

RACHEL

(Angrily) Jesus Christ!

CHRIS

Don't tell me you just met him now: here.
*(*RACHEL *heaves a deep sigh of exasperation, and sits down.* CHRIS *follows.)*

RACHEL

(Shaking her head) It's hopeless.

CHRIS

The way that chap smiled at me: that thin, snide smile —

RACHEL

(Sharply) That guy is anything but snide.

CHRIS

You know him quite well then, don't you?

RACHEL

Some people take five years to know; others, five seconds. *(Snapping her fingers)* Like that!

CHRIS

(Sarcastically) Love at first sight.

RACHEL

You're paranoid.

CHRIS

(Firmly) A paranoid whose instincts are never wrong.

RACHEL

These are hardly the words of a man who loves to wear his self-doubt on his sleeve.

CHRIS

So you think I'm some kind of Dr. Jekyll and Mr. Hyde?

RACHEL

It doesn't matter what I think.

CHRIS

It does to me. Very much. *(Emotionally)* I love you, Rachel; I do.

(He puts his hand over hers. She withdraws hers.)

RACHEL

But we keep having these rows. And they are getting worse. It worries me.

CHRIS

It worries me too, darling. *(Pause)* I think you should go to a psychiatrist.

RACHEL

Why should I?

CHRIS

Umm... it'd help... balance our relationship.

RACHEL

God! I'd have to go every day.

CHRIS

Not in the beginning. You can start with once a week.

RACHEL

Why start using a crutch I don't need?

CHRIS

It is not a crutch.

RACHEL

You can't tell. You've got so used to it you think it's a necessity.

CHRIS

But I've been without it since I went away filming four days ago.

RACHEL

And how do you feel?

CHRIS
(Sadly) Terrible, just terrible. And my back hurts.

RACHEL
Didn't the hotel give you the hard bed they promised?

CHRIS
You know the hotels in these places. They can't even produce a cup of coffee after dark, promise or not.

RACHEL
(With rising sympathy) Is it bad?
CHRIS
(Exaggerating) Very bad.
RACHEL
(Motherly) Poor darling! Now, if you turn around.
(CHRIS turns around. RACHEL, knowing the drill, starts to massage his back.)
It feels all knobbly.

CHRIS
Umm...

RACHEL
Did you have a bath everyday?
CHRIS
No. Not everyday.

RACHEL
But it has been so warm.
CHRIS
I know.

RACHEL
I thought you were coming back tomorrow evening.

CHRIS
Yes, by this afternoon, I was too tired to go on. It had been so warm and humid. I hadn't slept a wink for three nights... and I had no pills. By then I had finished everything except a few exterior shots. Well, Nick can take care of that.

RACHEL
You could have phoned.

CHRIS

It was seven by the time I decided to leave. I did phone but there was no reply. I had a flat on the motorway, in the pitch dark; and I had a splitting headache by the time I got home. And, to crown it all there was no damn coffee in the house.

RACHEL

I'm sorry, darling. I ran out of coffee this morning.

CHRIS

Oh, that's all right... not to worry... I'm sorry for having shouted at you. I was very exhausted after having battled with the egos and super-egos of a dozen actors for four days.

RACHEL

I did volunteer to come along, didn't I?

CHRIS

Yes, you did.
(Pause.)

RACHEL

You did see the telephone messages?

CHRIS

(Self-importantly) Yes, had a quick look *(Pause)* That'll do.
(RACHEL stops massaging.)
Thanks, darling.
(He turns around and moves close to her.)
Let's go.

RACHEL

Where?

CHRIS

Home. Where else?

RACHEL

But I have to wait.

CHRIS

What for?

RACHEL

The fags.

CHRIS

There must be some at home.

RACHEL

No, there aren't. Anyway, there's some money to be returned.

CHRIS

(Surprised) To whom?

RACHEL

Anwar.

CHRIS

What for? *(Angrily)* Why did you take money from this — this chap? Why?

RACHEL

Calm down.

CHRIS

I don't know what you're upto: Going off boozing with David — and whatever else? Then this character in the laundrette! And the money. And —

RACHEL

(Shouting) Will you shut up?

CHRIS

(Shouting) No! I won't!

(ANWAR arrives.)

ANWAR

(With a charming smile) I'm afraid the cigarette-machine is out of order.

CHRIS

(Abrasively) Don't lie. There's no cigarette-machine in the area.

(ANWAR is surprised by Chris's reaction, and forgets to return him the money.)

RACHEL

(Sharply) How do you know? You don't smoke.

CHRIS

(Subdued) I used to.

RACHEL

That was a long time ago.

ANAWAR

They keep moving these cigarette-machines around, you know.

CHRIS

(Limply) Oh, I keep track.

RACHEL

(Looking Chris *in the eye)* You do, do you?

CHRIS

(Avoiding her glare) Yes, I do.

RACHEL

You're a liar.

CHRIS

(Rationalising) Umm... One could say that... I lie... sometimes.

RACHEL

Sometimes?

CHRIS

For professional reasons... Umm... In my business one can't avoid lying to people... to get them to do what one wants them to...

ANWAR

(Genuinely curious) Is that what you do with your actors?

CHRIS

You're not an actor, are you?

ANWAR

No.

CHRIS

I didn't think so. *(Pretentious)* Actors are a breed by themselves: incorrigibly egocentric. They never give you what you want; so I lead them astray, misguide them all the time.

RACHEL

You're not going to misguide *me* any longer.

CHRIS

(Surprised) Why should I? You're not an actrees.

RACHEL

That's not the point. *(Bluntly)* You're dishonest: period. And you are dishonest with everybody. It's time somebody told you the truth.

CHRIS

(Hurt) In front of a stranger?

RACHEL

It's done, anyway.

CHRIS

Please return him *(indicating* Anwar*)* his money, so that we can go.

RACHEL

You go.

CHRIS

Aren't you coming with me?

RACHEL

I want to think it over.

CHRIS

But you were ready to leave only a few minutes ago.

RACHEL

I have the right to change my mind, don't I?

CHRIS

(Pointing to Anwar, *condescendingly)* For him?

(ANWAR steps forward.)

ANWAR

(Forcefully) Yes, for me. Why not?

CHRIS

Ah, well — *(With a knowing smile)* If only you knew the truth.

ANWAR

The truth? From you? That's a joke.

(He lets out a short, mocking laugh.)

CHRIS

(Scandalised) Do you know she is pregnant, by me?

RACHEL

(Upset) How did you know?

CHRIS

(Grinning victoriously) David told me.

RACHEL

Oh.

ANWAR

(To Rachel *mock acting)* That's a bit much to take for a man who isn't the father. *(To* Chris *with a superior grin)* I knew before you did.

CHRIS
(Looking lost) Oh. She has already told you then? How very noble!

ANWAR
(Firmly) Honest — is the word.

CHRIS
You mean, you don't mind her bearing my child while rejecting me, outright.

ANWAR
No. *(Matter-of-factly)* A child is the exclusive property of a woman.

CHRIS
(Flabbergasted) You're crazy.

ANWAR
Crazy enough to be rational, logical. A man provides no more than a speck of a sperm.

CHRIS
But: no sperm, no child.

ANWAR
Sperms are cheap. You get them by million, in one go. But wombs are not. And: no womb, no child.

CHRIS
You are suffering from a castration complex.
(ANWAR *laughs a loud, derisive laugh.*)
(Feeling crushed) Why did you laugh at me like that?

ANWAR
(Patronising) Ask your psychiatrist tomorrow.

CHRIS
Get off.
(Pause.)

ANWAR
Tell me, do you ever look anybody in the eye?

CHRIS
(Pretentious) An Englishman is taught, at a very young age, not to stare at people.

ANWAR
Don't I know — having grown up in England?

CHRIS

Oh, did you?

ANWAR

In Preston and London — *(quietly)* and Oxford.

CHRIS

I did think, for a moment, that you might be an Oxford type.

ANWAR

You're Cambridge, aren't you?

RACHEL

(Lightheartedly) And never the twain shall meet.

ANWAR

(Shakespearian) Except in battle.

RACHEL

In the arena of a London laundrette.

ANWAR

Without ever crossing glances.

CHRIS

(With some effort) I do look people in the eye if the situation so demands.

ANWAR

I doubt it.

CHRIS

(Irritated) What makes you so sure?

ANWAR

Okay. *(As a stray thought)* Look me in the eye.

CHRIS

What for?

ANWAR

Try it for size. Okay? Now, look me in the eye and say: 'You fuckin' wog'.

CHRIS

(Shocked) Why would I do a thing like that?

ANWAR

(With quiet authority) I said: look me in the eye, and say —

CHRIS

But wog is a word of abuse.

ANWAR

No, it isn't.

CHRIS

Umm...

ANWAR

It means a westernized oriental gentleman: w-o-g.

CHRIS

Oh?

ANWAR

(Loudly) Now, look me in the eye, and say, 'you fuckin' wog!' — you shit-bag!

CHRIS

No, I couldn't.

ANWAR

(Shouting) Say the fuckin' thing, and relieve yourself of your eternally constipated liberalism.

CHRIS

Christ... All right. *(Weakly)* You fuckin' wog.

ANWAR

Say it again: loud and clear.

CHRIS

(Hysterically) You fuckin' wog! You're stealing my girlfriend!

(ANWAR hits Chris – a quick, sudden blow – and stands back, defensively, with both fists in the air. Pause. CHRIS recovers.)

What did you hit me for?

ANWAR

You accused me of stealing your girlfriend. False. One can steal only what belongs to somebody else.

CHRIS

(Indicating Rachel) She belongs to me.

RACHEL

(Assertive) I belong to myself.

ANWAR

Amen!

CHRIS

(To Rachel; pathetically) Is that what I get, after all that I've taught you?

RACHEL

You sound like one of your actors: 'incorrigibly egocentric'.
(ANWAR punches the air)

ANWAR

(To Chris) Okay, okay. Come on, shit-bag. I'll teach you
something in return.
(Reluctantly, CHRIS takes up a boxer's position.)

CHRIS

Don't you goad me. I'm a slow boiler. But once I boil —
*(ANWAR takes a few jabs at CHRIS, who manages to parry,
stiffly.)*

ANWAR

(Sarcastic) Yes, I know. She has told me.
*(ANWAR again attacks CHRIS, who is still stiff. RACHEL is
rivetted by this.)*

CHRIS

This is not fair. I'm not trained for this.

ANWAR

Nor am I.

RACHEL

That makes you even. Ox versus Bridge.
*(CHRIS now shows some initiative, but still not enough.
ANWAR is keeping up the pressure.)*

ANWAR

Come on, you mish-mash!

CHRIS

Don't you call me that.

ANWAR

Come on, show your balls.
*(An excited RACHEL literally bites her nails as CHRIS and
ANWAR exchange a few light punches.)*

RACHEL

Wait.

CHRIS

What's the matter?

RACHEL

I must go for a pee.

CHRIS

Right now?

RACHEL

Yes!

CHRIS

Where?

RACHEL

I don't know. Any where... Here... if you turn off the lights.

ANWAR

No, no. *(Raising his right fist)* Okay, hold it. Break.

CHRIS

(Limply) Okay.
(ANWAR returns to a normal posture, and so does CHRIS.)

ANWAR

There must be a way.

RACHEL

Quick.
(CHRIS is disinterested while ANWAR looks around frantically. He points to the door marked 'Private'.)

ANWAR

There!

RACHEL

It's probably locked.
(ANWAR tries to push open the door but it is firmly locked.)

ANWAR

All we need is a wire or something.

CHRIS

That's illegal.
(ANWAR and RACHEL start looking for something to open the lock. RACHEL burrows into her handbag, and brings out a nail file.)

RACHEL

(To Anwar) Try this.
(ANWAR takes the nail file and tinkers with the lock.)

CHRIS

(Disapproving) Is that really necessary? All that is required is —

ANWAR

Action. Not words.

CHRIS

This is private property.

ANWAR

Fuck private property.
(He unlocks the door.)
(Gesturing) Open sesame!
(RACHEL proceeds to the door.)

RACHEL

(To Anwar*)* Thank you. *(To both)* Don't you do anything until
I get back.

ANWAR

As you say, Ms. Ali Baba.
*(RACHEL closes the door partly and disappears in the dark.
ANWAR and CHRIS stand, arm folded, staring at each
other warily. Tense moments. A relaxed RACHEL emerges,
and flashes a smile at each of them. Then like a sheep
farmer she puts her finger under the tongue, and whistles
loudly.)*

RACHEL

Okay. Five, four, three, two, one — Go!
*(ANWAR and CHRIS take up positions as boxers, with
CHRIS facing the entrance. They spar for a while. A
POLICEMAN enters. CHRIS sees him and stops prancing
about. RACHEL sees him too. But ANWAR with his back to
the entrance, continues to dance on his feet.)*

ANWAR

Come on. Let's see what you're made of.

POLICEMAN

What do we have here?
(He goes past Anwar *and faces him.)*
A Mohammed Ali in action?
(ANWAR freezes.)

ANWAR

(Recovering) Nothing, officer; nothing serious —

CHRIS

(Forcefully) Oh, this was *serious.* We — she and myself — we were just passing by when we saw this man *(indicating* Anwar*)* breaking open that door. So, we came inside, and —

ANWAR

(Hotly) Not true.

POLICEMAN

Please, Sir, let the gentleman finish.

CHRIS

(To the Policeman*)* You can check for yourself, officer. The door is marked 'Private'. And yet, right at this moment, you'll find it unlocked.

(The POLICEMAN *checks the door and finds it locked.)*

(Flustered) I could have sworn the door was open only a few moments ago. Ask her.

RACHEL

(To Chris*)* That's all right. You finish your story first.

CHRIS

(More flustered) We found him with what looked like a nail file in his hand, bending over, in front of the door. Didn't we, Rachel? *(Pause)* I'm sure you'll find it somewhere around here.

(He looks around.)

There.

(The POLICEMAN *notices the nail-file, and bends to pick it up.)*

Careful, officer. It has his *(indicating* Anwar*)* finger-prints on it.

(The POLICEMAN *puts the nail file on a washing machine.)*

POLICEMAN

(To Rachel*)* Who started the fight?

CHRIS

(Leisurely) We — that is, myself — challenged him. And he became violent and abusive. He called me a shit-bag; and what else? Oh yes — mish-mash — he called me that too. He began to hit me. So naturally I had to protect myself. Well, I had to — while she — she tried to phone 999.

POLICEMAN

(To Rachel*)* Did you, madam?

RACHEL

It's all a pack of lies.

CHRIS

She's *my* girlfriend. We live at 13A, Courtland Street, not far from here.

RACHEL

That may be true. The rest isn't. This gentleman here, Anwar Hassan — a law graduate and a travel agent — he and I have been in the laundrette for the past forty minutes or so. What that gentleman *(indicating* Chris*)* has just said is rubbish.

CHRIS

She's lying! She peed *(indicating)* behind that door.

POLICEMAN

She — what? — Sir?

CHRIS

(Frantic) Peed, passed water.

ANWAR

(To the Policeman; *legalistically)* Even if that were true, how could anyone prove it?

POLICEMAN

(To Chris; *sternly)* Now, Sir, you must be careful about making accusation of indecent exposure. *(To* Anwar*)* What do you have to say, Sir?

ANWAR

The lady here has said it all. I have nothing more to add.

CHRIS

(Protesting) They're both lying.

POLICEMAN

Well, Sir, I have the word of two against one. And, you did say that the lady is your girlfriend.

CHRIS

Yes, of course. You can see that she has no laundry of hers.

RACHEL

(To the Policeman*)* Nor has he. So, what's he doing here?

CHRIS

(To the Policeman*)* I'm waiting for her to come home with me.

RACHEL

(To the Policeman*)* I'm not going with him.

CHRIS

(To Rachel*; surprised)* Why didn't you say so before?

RACHEL

I did; but you took no notice.

CHRIS

(Conciliatory) Perhaps we could discuss this.

RACHEL

(Exasperated) God! Haven't we discussed enough?

CHRIS

Well, you know... after a good night's sleep... with clear minds in the morning.

RACHEL

(Firmly) Which will slide into their stale grooves by the afternoon.

CHRIS

(Hurtfully) How can you be so categorical?

RACHEL

Because of what has happened in the past.

CHRIS

One can always make a fresh start, you know.

RACHEL

We've tried that so many times, haven't we?

CHRIS

(Weakly) Yes.

RACHEL

But it hasn't worked.

CHRIS

Well, this time it might. *(Optimistically)* It will.

RACHEL

(Firmly) It won't. And, deep down in your heart, you know it.

CHRIS

(Unhappily) No, I don't.

RACHEL

I'm sorry, Chris, but we've reached the end. It's time to part.

CHRIS

Like this? Here?

RACHEL

(Gently) Better here, and now, than... And as friends, please.

CHRIS

You leave me with no other choice. *(Pause)* All right. *(To the Policeman)* Sorry about this, officer.

POLICEMAN

That's all right, sir.

CHRIS

Good night, luv.
(He takes her hand limply.)
Take care.

RACHEL

You too.
(CHIRS leaves.)

POLICEMAN

(To Anwar, *sternly)* A laundrette isn't a gym, you know.

ANWAR

I'm sorry. There was no harm done.

POLICEMAN

Be a bit more careful in future. *(Indicating the drier)* Are these your clothes?

ANWAR

Yes.

POLICEMAN

They look dry to me.

ANWAR

(Drily) Yes.
(ANWAR walks to the drier; the POLICEMAN prepares to leave.)

RACHEL

Good night, officer.

POLICEMAN

Good night, madam.

(The POLICEMAN *leaves.* RACHEL *walks to the drier.* ANWAR *takes a sheet out of the drier. Together, they start folding it.* RACHEL *stops and goes to her handbag.)*

RACHEL

Before I forget.

(She takes out three pound notes from her wallet.)

I won't need these now. *(Pause)* Would I?

ANWAR

Of course not.

CURTAIN

NOTES

NOTES

NOTES

NOTES

NOTES

NOTES

NOTES

NOTES